(Upper L to R) riverboat on Sacramento River and Tuscan Springs Hotel; (lower L to R) Maywood Hotel in Corning and a river ferry; (center) Cone & Kimball Clock Tower (artist Brent Tandy).

Tehama County Genealogical & Historical Society

PO Box 415, Red Bluff, CA 96080

(530) 690-0303

TCGHSPresident@gmail.com

TehamaCountyHistory.com

Stories pertaining to people, places, or events in Tehama County history based on original research, personal interviews, recollections, etc., are welcome. Articles can be submitted to Josie Smith by calling (530-591-3869), mailing (1 Coleman Court, Chico, CA 95926), or emailing (MemoriesEditor@gmail.com).

Authors must cite sources of facts and claims where applicable. We reserve the right to vet all submissions and edit for brevity, grammar, spelling, punctuation, structure, and content (i.e., correct errors in historical fact and add context if needed). Please contact the Editor for assistance. Deadline to submit articles is October 1.

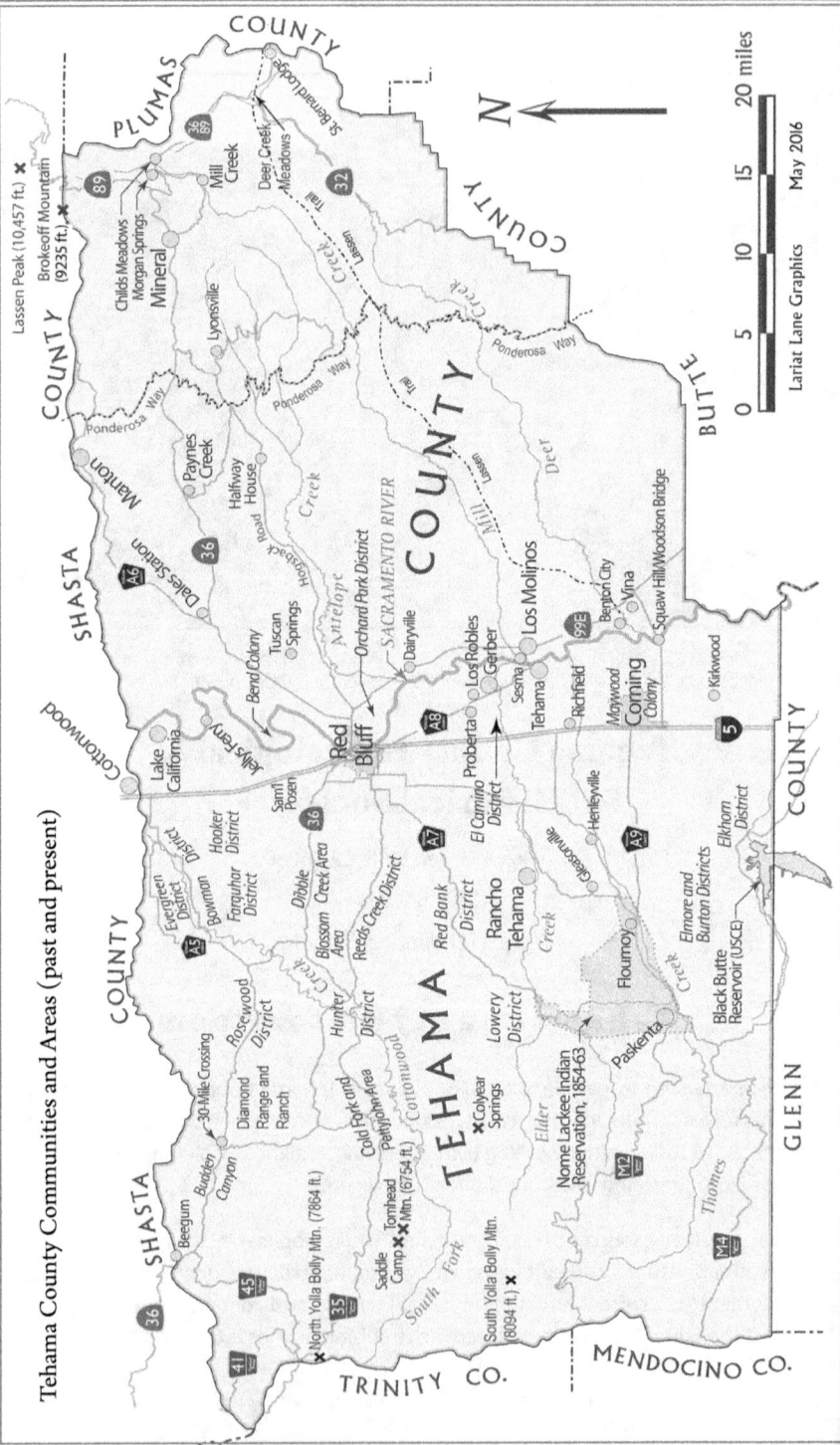

Tehama County Communities and Areas (past and present)

Lariat Lane Graphics   May 2016

0   5   10   15   20 miles

N

Our History is Best When You're Part of It!

Organized in 1980, the Society encourages valid research relating to the rich history and genealogy of our area, shares this history, and collaborates with individuals, clubs, organizations, the Tehama County Library, and local museums to collect and preserve items of historical and cultural significance.

The Tehama County Genealogical & Historical Society is strictly a volunteer-run non-profit of like-minded history nerds. Since 1980, we have, and continue to be, very serious about our mission of collecting, preserving, and sharing the history of Tehama County. It's very hard work, but well worth the effort.

Part of our work involves receiving and archiving donations given to us by individuals, families, or organizations. In 2024, we were honored to receive several important donations of Tehama County history. One such donation came from the **Tehama County Cattlewomen's Association**. After digitizing their significant collection of annual scrapbooks that stretched decades, they generously donated their scrapbooks to the Tehama County Genealogical & Historical Society for preservation and safekeeping. We also recently received copies of former Dairyville resident and author **Arla Gridley Farmer's** long out-of-print book, ***The Red Bluff Navy***, from her family who also kindly gave us permission to reprint this book in the future. You will find a short excerpt from her book and information about how to order a copy on page 66-68 in this issue of *Memories*. Our only funding comes from memberships, donations, and book sales. Every cent is dedicated to the ongoing effort of collecting, protecting, and fostering the history and genealogy of Tehama County.

We ask that you consider the Tehama County Genealogical & Historical Society when you are making decisions about what to do with history you've collected over the years. Too often, important local history gets tossed because family members aren't interested or don't have the bandwidth to preserve the items and information. Or, as we've heard too many times, no one knew who might want these types of items. ***We do. It's out mission. That's what we're here for.***

If you have stuff or questions about how to donate items to the Society, please contact me personally at **tcghspresident@gmail.com** or call **(530) 690-0303**.

We appreciate your continued support, and hope you enjoy the 2024 issue of *Memories*. So grab a cup of coffee or a cup of tea and enjoy this year's trip down memory lane!

~ Linda Severietti-Torres, President

Table of Contents

Pin Feather on the American Eagle
Albert Toomes (1817-1873)
Thomas E. Chavez

At first glance, there seems nothing particularly outstanding about the life of Albert G. Toomes. He never led armies on missions of conquest nor did he leave behind great tomes of thought. His name appears in few books of California history. Yet in another sense, Albert Toomes was most significant. His role in the fur trade, the Santa Fe Trail, early California settlement, the Mexican War, and community development in Tehama County must have been duplicated by countless others who were equally unknown. It was not without reason that the great proponent of expansion, Senator Thomas Hart Benton, of Missouri, once said that the United States claims to the Pacific Coast would eventually be validated by the American pioneers.[1] Here lies Toomes' importance: He was one of these pioneers, and when all their stories have been told, we will have a much better understanding of how Manifest Destiny actually worked in practice.

Albert Toomes was born in Missouri in 1817, the famous "jumping off" place for the lucrative fur trade, whose financial center lay in Saint Louis.[2]

Reprinted courtesy *The Pacific Historian*, Vol. 22, No. 2, Summer 1978 (pp. 173-,183) Holt-Atherton Special Collections, University of the Pacific, Stockton, CA.

He joined the trade in 1833, when he was only sixteen. 1833 is a memorable year in Western history for the greatest trapper of them all, Jedediah Smith, chose then to retire and try his hand in the Santa Fe trade. But on his way to the Mexican capital, when he stopped to look for water, Smith was killed in a Comanche ambush. That same year Albert Toomes crossed the plains on the trail on which Smith met his death.

After he arrived in Santa Fe, Toomes enlisted in his first fur trapping party, with Cyrus Alexander, a well-known trapper of the time. Alexander, Toomes, and five other men formed a party which officially was to trap in the interior states of Mexico. After they left Santa Fe, however, they followed an old custom and turned instead into the fur rich Gila Wilderness in southwestern New Mexico. Once there they were safe from the official arm of Mexico.

Eventually they moved down the Gila River to the Colorado River. When they reached the Colorado they realized they were only a short jump from the California settlements and they decided the coast might provide a better market than Santa Fe. This proved to be a disastrous decision. When they tried crossing the Colorado River, they lost all their goods. Thus, in late 1833 a bedraggled party of Americans arrived in San Gabriel, where they eventually dispersed.[3]

Toomes decided not to remain in California and soon returned to the states. But he had heard and seen things in New Mexico and California that he would retain for the rest of his life. Pushed on by his newly acquired knowledge and the promise of lucrative trade on the Santa Fe Trail, he became part of the early movement of manifest destiny and offered to lead overland parties to California.

As late as 1840, no immigrant party had ever gone overland to California. But, thanks to the many trappers who had explored the area, several routes had been established. In Missouri, a young man named John Bidwell, who had been swindled out of his land in Iowa, listened to the glowing descriptions of California from a trapper named Antonine Robidoux. Captivated by the old man's first-hand portrayals, Bidwell formed an immigrant society of people who intended to move west. This resulted in the Bartleson-Bidwell Party which gathered at Westport, Missouri, from whence they left in 1841.[4] Albert Toomes and Isaac Givens, another experienced man of western travel, had also formed a western caravan. They had hoped to join Bidwell but rode into Westport a few days too late. As a result, they decided they would not follow the departed group but would go another way, down the familiar Santa Fe Trail, instead. A caravan leaving for Santa Fe had the added benefit of security in numbers.[5]

As a result of a recent Texan Expedition to claim New Mexico for the new republic, however, Santa Fe proved to be an inhospitable place for Anglo-Americans. Many of the Anglo inhabitants had been accused of complicity with the Texans and the Toomes party arrived just at the apex of this turmoil.

Fearing for their families' lives, Toomes and several others met secretly at Abiquiu and made plans to flee for California. They quickly prepared buffalo meat "after the manner of trappers," and purchased provisions in Santa Fe, including 150 head of sheep.[6] Joining Toomes were Givens, Wade Hampton, and John McLure, all of whom had missed the Bidwell Party. In all, about twenty-five people left in early September for California.[7] Driving their sheep in front of them, they followed a regular New Mexican trade caravan led by Francisco Estevan Vigil.

Toomes and company enjoyed an uneventful journey. Pleased about escaping from turbulent New Mexico, they still remained unsure of what to expect from the officials in California. The travelers were reminded that previous sojourners were often not so fortunate when they crossed the dry Southwestern desert: carcasses of horses marked their way west.[8]

Vigil's caravan arrived in Los Angeles before Toomes' Party, known to history as the Roland-Workman Party. Vigil reported to the officials of the recent arrival of a group of settlers who intended to make their homes in California. The Governor sent Don Jose Castro to meet the foreigners, and he was told that they left New Mexico because of Indian problems.' In the list of names and occupations given to the Mexican official, Toomes listed himself as a carpenter.[10] Although he was only twenty-four years old, he had landed on the west coast for the second time in eight years. This was only the second group of pioneers to make the overland trip.[11]

As the settlers dispersed, Toomes moved to Monterey, California's capital, where he met Robert H. Thomes, another carpenter who had just arrived with Bidwell.[12] The two men formed a construction company which contracted work from the Bryant and Sturgess Company, a major New England institution along the California Coast. Toomes and Thomes

ROBERT HASTY THOMES.

erected several buildings to serve as hide-houses for the New England firm, which was then the only shipper of hides and tallow from Monterey.[13]

In 1844, Toomes followed many other California pioneers and became a naturalized Mexican citizen. Aside from any particular love for Mexico, there were advantages in such a move. Mexican citizenship made one eligible to receive a land grant.[14] If he were like the rest of the new arrivals, Toomes probably made this move with his eye on some nearby land.

Besides his carpentry, his early years in Monterey remained active. He soon became friends with all the important people in the area. He renewed his friendship with William Chard and Joseph Paulding, both of whom had been with him on his 1833 trapping adventure. He met Job F. Dye, who would become a lifelong friend. He also became friends with John Bidwell, then employed by John Sutter, who was proprietor of New Helvetia

Job F. Dye

John Bidwell (Bidwell Mansion SHP)

John A, Sutter, 1850 (CA State Library)

Peter Lassen

(Sutter's Fort) and with Sutter himself. On at least one occasion Toomes, Dye, Chard, and Peter C. Lassen, another life-time friend, joined Bidwell on a foray into the upper Sacramento Valley. Bidwell and Lassen had traversed the area in 1843 in pursuit of a party bound for Oregon which had allegedly stolen some of Sutter's horses. The horses were recovered and the men enjoyed the scenic beauty so much that Lassen selected some land for a future grant. He thus became the first settler north of Sutter's Fort. A year later Toomes and Dye were likewise impressed. They, too, petitioned the Mexican government for a grant.[15]

Sutter's Fort, 1849

Governor Manuel Micheltorena

The primary reason that Toomes and friends received their requested grants was that Governor Manuel Micheltorena's government was losing its popular support. Anxious about the increasing influx of Anglos in 1844, the governor made active attempts to gain support for his regime. He approved petitions for thirty-three land grants, which totaled over six hundred thousand acres in the Sacramento Valley, twenty grants of which were above the Feather River. Most of the grants were located on prime land along rivers or creeks, and they provided fertile soil and easy access.[16]

Toomes' acquisition of the 22,172 acre "El Rancho de los Molinos" grant was part of this. The grant was the end of a process that began with sending a petition and map to the Governor. Numerous procedural steps then followed: these included forwarding the petition to the Secretary of State (before his house was built, by Toomes and Thomes); verification by his friend Sutter that the land was vacant; a recommendation by the Secretary of State (after his house was finished); approval by the Assembly: and, finally, the approval of the Governor.[17]

Toomes and Dye quickly put their land to use. They formed a partnership in the cattle business. As early as 1845 the two men were driving their recently-purchased cattle to the upper Sacramento Valley for pasture. A steady market was available at Sutter's Fort. Both men utilized their grants in the livestock business, but since neither built a house, they appear not to have been in a hurry to live on their property.[18] They realized, however, that they had to use the land to retain it. Under the Mexican system of usufruct, they could not leave their new possessions in an idle state. Indeed, the government called on Bidwell and Reading to testify that the grants were, indeed, in use after 1845.[19] So much care was taken in these matters that Toomes, Thomes, Dye, and Chard went to their newly acquired property in November 1845, Toomes and Dye using the occasion to drive some cattle to Sutter's Fort.[20]

They stayed about two months; after establishing their presence, they left, for they all still maintained residences at the capital.[21]

As a resident of Monterey, Toomes continued his work as a carpenter, but not for long. In 1846, the United States declared war with Mexico, and California, especially Monterey, was a prime target. Commodore John P. Sloat of the United States Navy took the Mexican capital without firing a shot. Five days after the occupation of Monterey, the Commodore commissioned Captain Purser D. Fauntleroy to form a company of California Dragoons. Most of the volunteers were sailors anxious to get off their ships, but Albert Toomes also enlisted on July 12, 1846. The company consisted of a commander, two lieutenants, a guide, and the ordinary soldier. Toomes was commissioned a first lieutenant and Dye became the guide.[22] While the company saw no action against the Mexican forces, it did have a couple of skirmishes with Indians in the coastal mountains north of Monterey.

For the next two years, Toomes was busy running projects on his land and working in Monterey.[23] The cattle herds expanded to the point where the settlers had to institute some kind of control. Strays were a constant problem.[24] Since Toomes was spending so much time in the north valley, it appears he was preparing for an eventual move there. In 1846 he found time to build an adobe house on his ranch and shortly thereafter the area's first sawmill and gristmill were constructed.[25] The area even began to have a crime problem. Toomes was authorized by Larkin to look for any horses with his brand and leave them at his ranch, and, if they should come across a certain "Rimando [sic] Soto," they were to take him to John Williams, Larkin's hired hand. The area was suffering the birth pangs of civilization.[26]

Sometime before 1848, and after his service with Fauntleroy's Dragoons, Albert Toomes married a local woman, Maria Isabella. Unable to have children, they eventually adopted a daughter named Nellie Helen. Tragically, she later became afflicted with an incurable disease which made her incompetent. The couple apparently cared very much for each other for in 1848, while Toomes was on a gold hunting trip, Larkin received word to tell Maria Isabella "that Toomes has got quite well and can eat two men's allowance."[27]

He went prospecting in the spring of 1848. Among the men who partook in the expedition were Dye and Thomes. After six weeks they found enough gold to make $10,000 per man.[28] By October, the party split up in search of other locations along the Feather River.[29] Larkin, who remained in Monterey, appears to have been a major financial backer of the expedition. He later borrowed from some of the other forty-niners, but not Toomes, who had disposed of "nearly all his dust."[30]

Along with his new wealth and domestic status came local respectability. Although he had no formal schooling himself, Toomes was nominated to the board of trustees of a new school built in Monterey. Larkin charged the new trustees for Cotton Hall "to preserve it from wanton injury or unnecessary exposure."[31] This was an indication of the great respect Toomes must have had locally.

By 1849 the Toomes had moved permanently to their ranch. After this, he was to devote almost all his time to ranching. Unlike many of the neighboring grant owners, Toomes never was forced to sell his land to pay off any errant business deals. The property of Toomes, Dye, and Lassen covered most of the east side of the Sacramento River for about thirty miles north from Nord in Butte County. Toomes was one of the original settlers in what would become Tehama County.[32]

On March 3, 1851 the United States Congress passed an act entitled "An Act to Ascertain and Settle the Private Land Claims in the State of California." This was an attempt by the American government to deal with the many Mexican land grants. Such awards had to be confirmed. An official Federal Land Commission was formed to receive the claims and testimony. Toomes and his neighbors submitted their deeds in early 1852. No doubt his popularity made an impression, for Bidwell and Reading testified on his behalf. The hearings went so well Toomes wrote to Larkin that he received the decisions of the land commissioners and was "thankful." He was only sorry they left without doing more.[33] After word of Washington's acceptance of the various land petitions the *Red Bluff Beacon* reported that lands "are benefiting from the husbandmen owners," who have planted quantities of wheat. Their farms have the appearance of old settled Mid-western farms.[34] In December 1858, Toomes received his official patent.[35]

Toomes' land was planted with wheat and some fruit trees. He also started planting exotic flora, something for which he would later become famous.[36] The wheat or barley crops, however, became his mainstay and steadily increased his prosperity. In 1870 one observer noted that Toomes had twelve thousand acres devoted to wheat growing.[37]

1856 was a pivotal year for Toomes and his neighbors. He not only had a banner harvest, he also took part in the formation of Tehama County with its seat at the city of Tehama.[38] He was probably an original member of the County Board of Supervisors, perhaps even the first Board President. Elections were held every year and the *Beacon* praised Toomes for his first year's efforts. The out-going supervisors were congratulated for their performance which would be a model for "generations to come." Tehama was fortunate, the editorial continued, to have selected such "honest, capable, and faithful men." As for the future, the paper was optimistic. "Mr. Toomes, the President of the Old Board, is still retained on the new, and with his six years experience as Supervisor of Coluse [*sic*] and Tehama Counties, is peculiarly fitted and qualified to instruct his fellow members.[39] Toomes was a true father of Tehama County.

As with other developing frontier communities, the Masons played a primary role in Tehama's civic organization. The Masons were made up of local men who were often community oriented. Tehama was no exception. From its inception, the town had a "Molino Lodge," and Toomes, Chard, and Thomes were all Master Masons. They were instrumental in getting a charter from the Grand Masons of California. Even prior to their charter, the Masons paid for the construction of Tehama's school house. Toomes and Thomes donated the site on the corner of Third and "C" streets. In return, the Masons received exclusive use of the second story of the two story structure. The school doors opened in the spring of 1861.[40] Such

Town of Tehama Mason Lodge and school (current home of the Tehama County Museum)

activities were a boon to the community and there is little doubt that the school house would not have been built had the Masons not existed.

After respectability came "society," and in 1858 Thomes and Toomes formed a jockey club. This was patterned after the New York Jockey Club. Toomes was elected the first President by the initial twenty-eight members. They leased the Tehama Race Track from Thomes at their second meeting. The first day of races was scheduled for May 10, a day which brought warm weather, a big crowd and good races.[41] Racing became the most popular event of the county, but the purses rarely, if ever, exceeded one thousand dollars. Anyone could enter his favorite horse and every meet had at least one "grudge" match. On September 15, 1858, Toomes entered his horse "Bailey" in a grudge match for a thousand dollar purse. It was a "single dash of one mile."[42] Actually, the race proved no contest for the opposing horse "flew the track." Such unpredictable activity was normal for these events.

The *Red Bluff Beacon* publically urged the Jockey Club to expand into a county agricultural society. The editor claimed there was little benefit in finding out the fastest horse compared to the advantages of an agricultural society.[43] The Club never expanded, however, and Toomes apparently saw some use in the races. He even became a charter member in the nearby Red Bluff Jockey Club.[44]

Though the idea of an agricultural society was lost on the Club itself, it was well received by individual members. On February 6, 1861, Toomes and six other men were picked to draft rules for the organization of the Tehama County Agricultural Society. In a subsequent meeting Toomes was elected President.[45] The *Beacon* hailed the meeting as "a new era . . . dawning upon us.[46] A month later the paper took credit for the new organization: "Indeed this has been our measure, and we shall claim the honor of having put the ball in motion." It noted that the first meeting was composed of the best men and "heaviest" property holders in the county.[47]

The next step was political involvement and in 1860 Toomes' political career rose slightly. The Sacramento Valley was essentially a Democratic party area, and the local papers were so pro-Democrat they barely mentioned local Republican activities. In August 1860, the County Democratic Convention was to meet to elect representatives and create a platform for the state convention. Attending for the first time as a representative of the town of Tehama, Albert Toomes was elected to serve as one of the five delegates to attend the state convention. This modest achievement was the political apex of Toomes' career. He was re-elected to the County Convention in 1861, but did not represent Tehama in 1862.[48] If he had other political ambitions, they are not known.

The last years of Toomes' life were devoted to his many ventures, especially real estate speculation,[49] as well as his hobbies of hunting, gardening, and traveling. If his hunting trips resembled the trip he took to the coastal mountains in 1858, he was a very successful outdoorsman. On that outing, he and his friends captured eighteen deer, three elk, one bear and two hundred trout.[50]

One of his more enjoyable later day pastimes was to tell stories and reminisce with old friends. As an acquaintance later wrote, his tales were true to life, and he showed his love of beauty by "matchless descriptions" of his first view of the area. By this time he had built a mansion and surrounded it with gardens of exotic plants and trees. A full time German gardener was employed to help take care of the estate.[51] In such an environment, the amiable Toomes hosted his old trapper friends and fellow travelers from the Santa Fe and Old Spanish Trail days.[52]

On or around October 4, 1873, Albert G. Toomes passed away within sight of his beloved Elder Creek. He was 53. All his wordly possessions were left to his wife who survived until around 1880.[53] Ironically, the Tommes' name achieved what fame it did only after his death, for his wife's sanity was contested when she made her mark on her will. This case was appealed and in an 1880 land-mark decision, the California Supreme Court ruled that a Roman Catholic priest could testify as an expert. This proved to be a precedent making break in the legal barrier between Church and State in California jurisprudence.[54] Otherwise, however, Albert Toomes lived out his life in relative obscurity. He was but a pin feather on the nineteenth-century American Eagle that screamed. ◉

ENDNOTES

1. England and the United States claimed the Oregon Territory, both asserting prior occupation. See Frederick Merk, *The Oregon Question: Essays in Anglo-American Diplomacy and Politics* (Cambridge: Balknap Press of Harvard University Press, 1967).

2. As listed at the Bancroft Library, Berkeley, University of California, Peter E. Hanff, Coordinator-Technical Services to the Author. October 5, 1976.

3. Donald C. Cutter and David J. Weber, "Cyrus Alexander," *Mountain Men and The Fur Trade of the Far West*, Vol. 5 edited by LeRoy H. Hafen, (Glendale: The Arthur H. Clark Co., 1968), p. 28; *The Taos Trappers: The Fur Trade in the Far Southwest, 1540-1846*, (Norman: University of Oklahoma Press, 1971), p. 152.

4. The background to the Bartleson-Bidwell Party is found in many secondary sources, all largely based on the account of John Bidwell. *Echoes of the Past* (New York: Arno Press, 1973).

5. Bidwell, p. 42; David Lavender, *Bent's Fort*, (Lincoln: University of Nebraska Press 1972), p. 213.

6. LeRoy Hafen and Ann W. Hafen, *The Old Spanish Trail: Santa Fe to Los Angeles* (Glendale: The Arthur H. Clark Co., 1954), p. 207.

7. Marco Newmark, "The Workman Family In Los Angeles," *Southern California Quarterly*, Vol. 32 (December 1950), p. 316; Bidwell, pp. 41-42; Hafen, p. 207.

8. Hafen. p. 211.

9. Ibid, p. 213.

10. Newmark, p. 316.

11. Many of the Roland-Workman Party would go on to become prominent citizens in California. The Rolands and Workmans became influential citizens in the Los Angeles area. Included among the settlers was Los Angeles' first mayor and first Jew. See Max Vorspan and Lloyd P. Gartner, *History of the Jews of Los Angeles* (San Marino: The Huntington Library, 1970), p. 4. Some of the misconceptions about the expedition are that the route traveled through the Gila, as Toomes did in 1833. See Bidwell, p. 42. Another myth is that only Americans were in the party. There were two Mexican families and another man who brought servants. Women were included among the group. See Newmark, p. 316.

12. *Tehama County, California: Illustrations of Descriptions of Its Scenery, etc ... With Historical Sketches of the County* (San Francisco: Elliott and Moore, 1880), p. 109.

13. Drury Clifford, "Walter Colton, Chaplin and Alcalde," *California Historical Quarterly*, Vol. 35 (June 1956), p. 110; Bidwell, p. 48; *Tehama County ... Illustrations*, p. 109.

14. Lewis McCoy, "Land Grants and Other History of Tehama," (Unpublished paper, Tehama Public Library), p. 3; Clifford, p. 110. Another method with the same ends was to marry a Mexican girl.

15. Gertrude Steger, compiler, "A Chronology of the Life of Pierson Barton Reading," *California Historical Quarterly*, Vol. 22 (December 1943), p. 366; McCoy, p. 1.

16. Joseph A. McGowen, *History of the Sacramento Valley*, Vol. I, (New York: Lewis Historical Publishing Co., 1961), p. 35.

17. Clifford W. Penner, "Mexican Land Grants in Tehama County" (Unpublished Masters thesis, Chico State College, Chico, California). p. 46 has a chart which shows the procedure occurred from October through December 1844. This conflicts with Abel Steam's letter. Abel Stems to Thomas O. Larkin, November 27, 1845, *The Larkin Papers*, Vol. IV edited by George P. Hammond (Berkeley: University of California, 1953.) However, this does not conflict with the Governor's issuance of grants in 1844. Citation for acreage is McGowan, p. 36. Penner, p. 87 has a second chart which shows the Molinos' claim was granted in December. 1844. See also McCoy, p. 1, and Steger, p. 366.

18. Margaret C. Bauer, "History of Los Molinos Land Company and Early Los Molinos," (unpublished Masters thesis, Chico State College, Chico, California), p. 5; "John A. Sutter to Larkin, November 5, 1845," *Larkin Papers*, Vol. IV (Berkeley: University of California Press, 1953), p. 89.

19. Penner, p. 58.

20. Ibid, p. 52; "Sutter to Larkin, November 5, 1845," *Larkin Papers*, Vol. IV, p. 89.

21. Fred B. Rogers, "Bear Flag Lieutenant, Henry L. Ford," *California Historical Quarterly*, Vol. 29 (1950), p. 135.

22. George Walcoll Ames, Jr., "Horse Marines: California, 1846," *California Historical Quarterly*, Vol. 18 (1939), p. 82. The promotion reflects Toomes' experience and knowledge in California. It might also indicate his ability to handle people. An example of his patience is evident in "William F. Swasey to Larkin, June 23, 1846," *Larkin Papers*, Vol. V (1955), pp. 68-9. Swasey related how Toomes was effective in handling a "cantakerous customer" with the sale of wood.

23. McCoy, p. 8; Bauer, pp. 5-6.

24. "Talbot H. Green to Larkin, October 15, 1848," *Larkin Papers*, Vol. VIII (1962), p. 53.

25. McCoy, p. 8; Bauer, pp. 5-6.

26. "Larkin to Job Dye and Toomes, May 15, 1848," *Larkin Papers*, Vol. VII, (1960), p. 359.

27. "Talbot H. Green to Larkin, October 15, 1848," *Larkin Papers*, Vol. VIII (1962), p. 14.

28. Rogers, p. 54.

29. "Green to Larkin, December 2, 1848," *Larkin Papers*, Vol. VIII (1962), p. 14.

30. "Williams to Larkin, December 2, 1848," *Larkin Papers*, VIII (1962), p. 53; "Dye to Larkin, September 14, 1848," *Larkin Papers*, VII (1960), p. 359.

31. Drury, p. 110.

32. E.J. Lewis, *Tehama County, California* (San Francisco: Eliott & Moore, 1880), pp. 1, 8.

33. "Toomes to Larkin, August 30, 1852," *Larkin Papers*, Vol. IX (1963), p. 123.

34. *Red Bluff Beacon*, April 1, 1857, p. 2.

35. Penner, p. 87; McCoy, p. 3.

36. Clara Hough Hisken, *Tehama, Little City of the Big Trees* (Exposition Press, 1948), p. 20.

37. Bauer, p. 13.

38. McCoy, p. 8; Penner, pp. 8, 9.

39. *Red Bluff Beacon*, September 23, 1857, p. 2; May 27, 1857, p. 1; Penner, p. 58.

40. Don Jaselium, "History of Molino Lodge, Tehama," (Unpublished paper, Tehama County Library, Red Bluff), p. 2; Penner, p. 59; *Tehama County, Index to Deeds, Grantor and Grantee*, Vol. I, 1856-1874, May 13, 1868, Book F, p. 518. Hereafter cited *Tehama County Deeds*.

41. *Red Bluff Beacon*, March 17, 1858, p. 2; May 12, 1858, p. 2.

42. *Red Bluff Beacon*, September 15, 1858, p. 2.

43. *Red Bluff Beacon*, September 15, 1858, p. 2; September 22, 1858, p. 2; March 30, 1859, p. 2.

44. *Red Bluff Beacon*, May 2, 1861, p. 2.

45. *Red Bluff Beacon*, March 13, 1861, p. 2.

46. *Red Bluff Beacon*, May 2, 1861, p. 2.

47. *Ibid*, March 13, 1861, p. 2.

48. *Red Bluff Beacon*, August 29, 1860, p. 2; May 30, 1861; p. 2; August 14, 1862, p. 2; Penner, p. 58.

49. *Tehama County Deeds*.

50. *Red Bluff Beacon*, August 25, 1858, p. 2.

51. Lewis, n.p.

52. Hafen and Hafen, p. 218. Given's visit proved beneficial to piecing together the story of the role of the pioneer in American expansion. Toomes kept track of their fellow travelers in the Roland-Workman Party and passed the information to Givens who wrote it down. Also John Adam Hussey, "New Light Upon Talbot H. Green," *California Historical Quarterly*, Vol. 18 (1939), p. 56. In a broken down state, Givens found repose among his friends Toomes, Reading, Thomes and Dye. He spent a year with them.

53. Hisken. p. 20; Lewis, n.p.

54. Estate of Toomes, p. 509; Ronald Nelson, "The Legal Relationships of Church and State in California," *Southern California Quarterly*, Vol. 46 (March 1964), p. 21.

Bohemia Hop Ranch, south of Los Molinos, owned by the E. Clemens Horst Company. In 1933 a Japanese family occupied the small house on the left. To the right of the small house are the hop buildings (Opal Thornton Mendenhall collection).

The Japanese in Tehama County

Tehama County Genealogical & Historical Society

The first Japanese in Tehama County are believed to have been brought here by the Stanford Vina Ranch in 1895 to pick grapes. A Japanese contractor, T. Heroti, brought about 300 workers to pick about 15,000 tons of grapes at 90 cents per ton. Some Japanese were used in harvesting in subsequent years, along with Chinese and whites, until 1914, when most of the vineyard was taken out. Some of the Japanese were employed the year around. The Japanese and Chinese each had their own labor camp some distance south of the ranch headquarters. It is believed that all of the Japanese workers left after the final harvest in 1914.

The anti-Chinese movement in the county, which started in the 1870s and continued through the 1900s, extended also to the Japanese. In Corning in 1900 a group of whites threatened violence to a group of Japanese laborers unless they left town, which they did. Similar expulsions undoubtedly occurred elsewhere in the county and region but were not reported, probably because the methods used were outside the law.

Other than the Stanford Ranch workers, there have never been many Japanese in the county in the past. U.S. Federal Census records indicate that the number of Japanese living in the county were 140 in 1900, 98 in 1910, 107 in 1920, and 75 in 1930. The old timers remember several families previously located here. In the early 1900s the Star Laundry was operated on the southwest corner of Main and Oak streets by the families of I. Tomita and K. Iwao. When this business was destroyed by fire in 1910, the owners gained much respect by making good on all losses of laundry. By 1920 the Star Laundry was again operating at 828 Main Street.

In 1932 a large Japanese family lived and worked on the E. Clemens Horst Company hop farm, also known as the Bohemia Ranch, located between the railroad tracks and the Sacramento River. After work on the farm was finished for the day, the family repaired radios for people in a little shed near their house. They were also ham radio operators and would contact relatives in Japan. The family was gone by 1939.

There were also two Horst Company hop farms in Gerber, known as the Elder Creek and Shasta Farms. Two Japanese families who worked there were the Okomoto family, consisting of Harry, Taddy, and Mary; and the Ben Hiranoka family, Tama, Shamica, George, and Jimmy. After the declaration of war on Japan in 1941 these families were evacuated to relocation centers.

In June 1942 Hiroshi Kamiya operated the Star Laundry in Red Bluff. In July 1942 the family was evacuated to Tulelake, losing their business and the laundry was closed. Two other Japanese families living in Antelope Valley were also evacuated, probably to Tulelake. One family is known to be the Takashitas. In late June 1942 it was necessary for Paul Takashita to obtain special permission from the FBI to cross into a "military zone" so he could register for the selective service at the post office in Red Bluff. Within two weeks the family was relocated. [There was much paranoia regarding the Japanese-Americans following the bombing of Pearl Harbor, which explains the whole relocation program]. The other Japanese family evacuated was that of Itsuji Yokohari. His son Roy had just graduated from Lincoln Street School.

Some compensation for property losses for Japanese-Americans as a result of the relocation program in 1942 was paid in 1948, but many internees were unable to fully recover their losses. In 1988 the United States government officially apologized for the internment of Japanese-Americans during World War II and provided reparation payments of $20,000 for each surviving detainee.

Today there are many people in Tehama County with Japanese ancestry, as is true for all of California and the West Coast. The largest Japanese-American-owned business in the county is probably the 6,500-acre Masami Cattle Ranch near Corning, which was founded in 1988. It maintains about 5,000 to 8,000 head of cattle and operates a Wagyu breeding program. ◎

Sources

Tehama County Genealogical & Historical Society's *150 Years of Tehama County History*, available at TehamaCountyHistory.com.

"Masami Cattle Ranch" (masamiranch.com).

The east side of the 800 block of Main Street in Red Bluff. Left to Right: 1. Montgomery Ward and Co., 2. Empty lot except for Pet Milk billboard, 3. unknown business, 4. Star Laundry. The Hiroshi Kamiya family owned the Star Laundry at the time of this picture, ca. 1930. (Bayles collection).

18

Lost Mine on Your Doorstep

William "Old Hutch" Hutchinson

The legend of Peter Lassen's Lost Mine is as old as the first white settlement he made in the valley north of New Helvetia where Deer Creek breaks from the hills to cross the Vina Plains and reach the rolling Sacramento. The legend of Obe Leininger's Ledge is a little younger for Obe Leininger was a seeker after the Lost Mine whose stories had been part and parcel of his youth—the tales told around the hearth of a winter evening in the days before good roads, radio, television and picture magazines.

The foothill Indians of that region, the Yahi, gained an evil reputation amongst the early settlers for their acquired taste for ox and mule meat, for their skill at homicide and evasive tactics. Yet these same Indians, when opportunity afforded, were wont to bring in coarse gold to trade at the settlements of Hall's Ferry (Tehama), Monroeville, and other river towns long since gathered into the sea. Since Peter Lassen treated these people as people, not as vermin, he was reputed to know and use their secret trove. Moreover, in 1850, an educated emigrant, J. Goldsborough Bruff, who was surveying a town site for Lassen and "General" John Wilson, made certain entries in his diary: "June 18 In the afternoon Lassen and Dexter started out for the hills a short distance: July 2 At daybreak Lassen and Dexter returned

Lassen had some fine samples of gold he found." This same diarist noted, also, that when Lassen was robbed by an emigrant he had befriended, they had to weigh the dust on recovery to see if Uncle Peter had gotten back all that he had lost.

So the stories of Lassen's private gold supply flourished during the years he lived in the valley and after. That Lassen was forever in financial difficulties, that he died, far out in the Black Rock Desert of Nevada, seeking the Lost Hardin Mine, and still not wealthy—these facts were not enough to still the legend. Facts never are if the legend speaks of deep human hopes.

The legend gained a new lease on life almost twenty years after Lassen's death in 1859, when little spits of snow hissed against the brush in Deer Creek canyon and swirled into the eyes of Obe Leininger as he swung up his miner's pick and buried it deep in the trunk of the tree beside him. This was his way of marking the ledge of gold-flecked quartz he had just found against the day when he could return and stake his claim according to law. He could not stay in the moment of success lest the snow block him and his partner in until their scant provisions were exhausted.

Whether Obe Leininger found Lassen's Lost Mine or made a new find for himself is immaterial. What matters these days is simply that Leininger's Ledge is truly a lost mine on your doorstep, as close as the ignition switch in the family car and the freedom of vacation time.

You can base your search at a Forest Service campground beside the cold, clear crystal waters of one of California's better trout streams. You reach this haven, or go out for supplies after you get there, over State Highway 32, amidst magnificent Sierran scenery. If this sounds remarkably like the pre-election promises of an aspiring candidate, the best way to disprove it is to see for yourself.

State Highway 32 lifts you out of the Sacramento Valley at Chico by one of the most spectacular, ridgespine ascents in all the foothills. The highway follows, generally, the course of the Humboldt Road, an artery of commerce between California and southwestern Idaho in the Sixties, to Forest Ranch and on to Lomo where the Humboldt Road goes right to the summer homes of heat- sick valley residents at Butte Meadows and Jonesville.

Your road, State Highway 32, swings left at Lomo, snaking around the canyons and ridge ends that feed Big Chico creek, until it crosses the Deer

Creek watershed and descends past Windy Cut, where it is good manners to stop at the Ranger Station to register and get a Fire

Permit. Below Windy Cut, the highway crosses Deer Creek by a bright, silvery bridge and a matter of a mile more brings you to the Potato Patch campground—stoves, tables, water faucets and wood for the cutting. There are other Forest Service camps in Deer Creek canyon but Potato Patch is best for your purposes. Your distance from Chico is a long forty miles; your distance from supplies, Auto Club services and hot-and-cold indoor conveniences is a scant thirty miles to Mineral, gateway to Lassen National Park, or to Chester and Lake Almanor. You can get on the ground quicker and easier than did Obe Leininger.

Leininger came back to the Vina Plains where he had been reared, from working in the Montana mines. His brother, John Leininger, was ranching there and after his homecoming had been accomplished, Obe Leininger decided to exercise the daemon that had long ridden him by looking for Peter Lassen's Lost Mine. He propositioned a neighboring rancher to side him in the search but this man, too, was busy with the jobs of running a ranch and feeding a family—the responsibilities of marriage and land left no time for feckless wayfaring. Obe Leininger and another bachelor, Spence Brown, were the two who set out with one pack-horse, Johnnie, up the old Lassen Trail out of the valley along the great ridge that separates the canyons of Deer Creek and Mill Creek. They worked their way well up the ridge, into the stand of ponderosa called Lassen's Pinery, making their headquarters at what was known to them as Lost Camp.

It took them several days to prospect the precipitous slopes running down from Lost Camp towards the canyon. Then, plunging into the gore of the canyon itself, above the deep indentation called Wilson's Cove, they found a great ledge of gold-bearing quartz where two small ravines forked. They built location markers of loose boulders and with the snow making an unmistakable threat, Obe Leininger drove his pick into the nearest tree and he and Spence Brown started to get out.

They did not know that they were lost until nightfall, when they realized they were stepping in their own boottracks. Next day, they tried again, rimming out of the canyon by main strength and blind instinct, until they came upon a familiar landmark, a rock in the form of a "4," that marked a trail into Deer Creek canyon from what they knew as Obe Field's Camp on the Lassen Trail. From this landmark, they found their camp, fed Johnnie a bait of oak leaves and headed down the trail for the Vina Plains and home.

They spent one night on their way back at the ranch of Thomas Benton Polk, the man Obe had asked to side him on the search. One of the Polk youngsters, Martin, remembers Obe Leininger chaffing his father for not coming with him and Martin Polk remembers, too, the specimens that he saw in Obe Leininger's hands in the mellow, yellow lamplight of long ago. "Good rock," Leininger called them, and he never made any other claim for the ledge he found and lost save this—"Good rock!" But Martin Collins Polk, trained engineer, long-time Assessor of Butte County, familiar spirit of mines real and mines imaginary in all the northern Sierra, has himself found evidence that Obe Leininger was not lying about the quartz ledge in Deer Creek canyon, even though Obe Leininger could never find his ledge again.

This came about in 1907 when Martin was bucking the Oro Light & Power Company for a water right in Deer Creek canyon. Running a flume-line grade upstream from his family's summer grazing homestead at Polk Springs, Martin found his head-gate site to be at the mouth of Calf Creek, just half a mile below the silvery bridge that carries State Highway 32 across Deer Creek below Windy Cut today. Here, he found quartz float. He does not say that it was shot with stringers, heavy with gold—he is too honest to salt himself—but it was promising.

However, Martin was then too intent upon the latent wealth in the waters of Deer Creek to follow up his float. Today, forty-seven years later, Martin Polk is still too busy to go a'seeking after Leininger's Ledge. Someday, perhaps, when he really retires, he may look on the side hill to the left of State Highway 32, between the mouth of Calf Creek and Potato Patch campground. Somewheres in there should be the ledge that spawned the float he found so many years ago. Perhaps the same ledge that loaded the gravel sluiced out by the Jackson and Occidental mines in Deer Creek canyon in the middle-eighties. *Quien Sabe?*

In all the years that have passed since that snowspitting day, no one has yet found the quartz ledge beneath the pick-marked tree. A resident of Los Angeles, Mr. C. F. Carlson, spent twenty summers seeking Leininger's Ledge and never found it. Standing on the butt end of a ridge, where the Campbellville Lookout perches, a logger named Laurence Blunkall has looked out across the Devil's Den to Wilson's Cove and the whole tangled complex of Deer Creek drainage and knows that his father found the pick-marked tree in there somewhere. His father was riding for cattle in that country, a newcomer he was and did not know the local legends including the significance of that pick-marked tree, and when he had learned them he could never go back to it again.

And once when Martin Polk was serving Chico as City Engineer, a stranger came to his office one fine morning and requested Martin's help. The man had found Obe Leininger's ledge, so Martin heard him say, while on a hiking trip in Deer Creek, and he needed Martin's knowledge to locate it properly. He had the geology of the canyon down pat; he had the geography of the canyon down pat; every question Martin asked him brought a reasonable answer. Martin Polk's interest increased accordingly until the lucky finder remarked that it was only by luck that he had spotted the pick, because in the years that had passed since Obe Leininger drove it there, the tree in growing had carried the pick up many, many feet into the air. Martin then decided that he was too busy to go wandering around Deer Creek canyon with a man who did not know that trees grow from the top up, not the bottom.

So, Leininger's Ledge and Lassen's Lost Mine, be they the same or different, are still where their finders left them—handy to the highway, to clear mountain water, and to trout. If you seek them in vain, it may be that the search will bring you other and more lasting values. It has done so to at least one seeker who is unnamed here. ◎

❧

"Old Hutch" was a master wordsmith, possessed with a fantastic memory for the details of history, and with a very extensive, as well as colorful, vocabulary. Accuracy was his guide, and truth was his creed in all his work as teacher and historian. A native of Denver, Colorado, he acquired a strong interest in the history and the folklore of the American West as he traveled through the Southwest states. He spent some youthful years as a horse wrangler and would-be cowboy in Arizona; also worked as a fireman, both stationary and locomotive; and mucker in mines, and harvest hand in California, Nevada, and Arizona. In 1964 he was invited to join the history Department at Chico State College as a Lecturer on a one-year temporary appointment. He remained a member of the faculty until his retirement in 1978 as a full Professor with Emeritus designation.

Source: *Tales From "Old Hutch": Selected Stories from Notebooks of the Old West* (available at TehamaCountyHistory.com)

Ostrich plucking announcement (*Los Angeles Evening Express*, March 16, 1905). Ostriches were plucked twice a year. In 1888, a good bird could yield $60 a year in feathers; 50 birds could yield $3,000 (approx. $100,000 today).

MAY LOCATE OSTRICH FARM.

Special to the Union.

RED BLUFF, March 14.—The Red Bluff ostrich farm, which has been taking up the attention of the boosters of Tehama's county seat for some time, probably will be located at the south end of the Walton subdivision, where the ground is rough and broken. Fifteen or twenty acres, in full view of passing trains and highway traffic, are said to be available. Twenty birds can be purchased for $700, and the cost of the houses and other necessary improvements would not be great.

Ostrich Farming in the Cold, Frozen North

Josie Reifschneider-Smith

In January 1879, a pound of ostrich feathers from South Africa sold for $860, or $8 a feather ($250 a feather in today's dollars). With single ostriches able to yield 100 feathers a year, this caused some $eriou$ interest in raising ostriches to supply a ready market with their plumes. In 1888, Tehama County's first ostrich farm was located a few miles north of Red Bluff on 2,100 acres along the Sacramento River when Dr. Charles J. Sketchley began moving his birds there from the Los Angeles area. He believed that Tehama County's climate would suit his ostriches well.

Sketchley started the first ostrich farm in Southern California in 1883, but rapid land development caused him to consider relocating. When word got out that he was heading north, the Los Angeles Times claimed the move to "Red Bluff, in Tulare County" was "fake" and that the "birds will remain in Los Angeles county. The Red Bluff boomers should now insert their heads into the sand and leave their brains exposed."

Newspapers around the state published this sentiment in one form or another, so it didn't take long to reach the Red Bluff Weekly Sentinel, which thundered back: "The people of Red Bluff are not alarmed at the last kick made by Los Angeles to save its dying fortunes. It's no wonder that in the throes of death it strikes at the cold, frozen north it has often maligned and whose rich lands, admirable climate, and unparalleled advantages it has lied about."

Despite the war of words, the ostriches settled well into their new home, enjoying fresh grass, alfalfa, corn, oats, and barley. When some escaped, they would be rodeoed like cattle back to the farm. Once, a male ostrich got out of its pen and headed straight for the Sacramento River. While Sketchley and his hired help followed by horse, the bird jumped in the river and swam to the other side first to Kraft's place and later to Fish & Jelley's ranch where it was driven into a corral. Once notified that "his lordship from Africa" had been captured, the doctor brought his bird back home, which didn't seem the least "disturbed by the long run and two baths." (Sketchley couldn't ferry his bird over the river because the Jelley's ferry had sunk a few days earlier.)

Within a year, Sketchley had moved his birds to another area, possibly to Santa Cruz. According to some accounts, it was because the winter that year had been unseasonable cold, which killed several birds. This effectively ended ostrich farming in Tehama County.

But it didn't end the interest in ostriches. In 1915, the Red Bluff Chamber of Commerce floated the idea of having a small ostrich farm. It created a lot of excitement, but the problem was where to put it—in town or nearby. It was suggested to put it in the newly developed Walton subdivision, across from Brewery Creek, north of town. Only 15 or 20 acres (possibly donated by the Walton Bros., the subdivision developers), a 7-foot fence, and a few sheds would be all the improvements needed for 20 birds. It would be in full view of passing trains and be a 10-minute walk to the Southern Pacific Depot. What better way to advertise Red Bluff and Tehama County? Best of all, the scheme would pay for itself because the town could make money by plucking feathers for a profit of $25 per bird. Several meetings were held and enthusiasm was high for the idea. However, demand for ostrich feathers declined before this thought could become a reality. ◉

Charles Brownstein, the Pioneer Baby Grave. Undated photo/author's collection.

Lonely Pioneer Baby Grave

Josie Reifschneider-Smith

About a mile west of old Shasta on Highway 299W (Shasta County) is Historical Marker #377 that marks the 1864 infant grave of Charles Brownstein, son of Red Bluff residents George and Helena Brownstein. Little Charles was 8 months old when he died. The heartbroken Brownsteins wanted their son buried in a Jewish cemetery. The closest one was in Shasta County, established in 1857 by the Shasta County Hebrew Congregation.

Memory of the little grave faded until rediscovered in 1923 by surveyors mapping the new Redding-Eureka highway (later Highway 299W). Old timers were consulted, but no one knew anything about the grave. Many believed it was that of an infant who had died in the wilderness along the California-Oregon pack trail during the Gold Rush.

Regardless of the mystery, the grave presented a problem for the surveyors. To their dismay, their planned route would go right over the grave. Instead of disinterring the grave, "they studied their blueprints and road maps, and then, with no one's permission, altered the course of the road a bit to one side so that the grave might remain undisturbed" (Sacramento Bee, May 29, 1933).

Helena Cohn Brownstein, mother of Baby Charles (no date). Her brother, Kaspare Cohn founded Cedars of Lebanon Hospital in 1902, which later merged with Mount Sinai Hospital in 1961 to become Cedars-Sinai Medical Center, Los Angeles, California.

For the next ten years, cars sped by the guardrails that protected the rusted wrought iron fence that enclosed the little grave with its chipped and weathered headstone that read: "Charles Brownstein, son of George and Helena Brownstein of Red Bluff. Born April 6, 1864. Died December 14, 1864."

In May 1933, a dedication was held to make the gravesite a permanent historical monument to pioneer days in Shasta. Two hundred people attended and speeches reinforced the mistaken belief that the baby died along the trail. But a week later, the Record Searchlight reported that two elderly ladies came to see the grave. They were the sisters of little Charles who was their older brother. They had been told by their parents that their brother was buried "somewhere in Northern California" but couldn't remember where or the reason why. Learning about the dedication led them to his resting spot. An agreement was made with the Shasta County Historical Society that if the society would care for the grave, they would not remove their brother to the family plot in Colma. They also arranged to have wreaths placed perpetually on the grave.

In 1947, the little grave was threatened again. The highway needed to be modernized. But this time, that segment of the old road was abandoned and the new route built nearby. Forty-one years later, in July 1988, the Record Searchlight reported that the gravestone had been stolen. BLM

archaeologist Dr. Eric Ritter called it a "real oddball kind of crime"
and major loss as the gravesite is the oldest Jewish burial site north of
Sacramento. The $300 reward offered by Secret Witness of Shasta County
led to the arrest of a 19-year-old Shasta man when the stone was found in
his house. A new stone and dedication ceremony took place in June 1989.

But who were George and Helena Brownstein, parents to little Charles?
According to Find-a-Grave, George emigrated to California from Germany
by ship and crossed the Isthmus of Panama by mule in 1850. He opened
a dry goods/clothing store on the corner of Main and Oak Streets in
Red Bluff (and throughout California) and met his future wife Helena
Cohn during a buying trip to San Francisco. Their first son (first name
unknown) made news four weeks after his birth in 1862 when the Red
Bluff Independent announced that he had undergone the Jewish rite of
circumcision, the first to have ever taken place in Red Bluff. ◉

WE DONT HAVE TO PRAY FOR RAIN AT LOS MOLINOS, CALIF.

Two postcards showing different dams on Mill Creek
(top: J. Smith personal collection; bottom: Tehama County Library archives)

AMOUS OLD MILL DAM AT LOS MOLINOS, WHICH ALSO DIVERTS WATER FOR IRRIGATION

Douglas Cone (1865-1905) about 1890. He and engineer Wayne Meredith made the first known hydropower proposal on Mill Creek in 1900 (Tehama County Library archives).

The Oro Water, Light & Power Company and Other Past Hydropower Plans for Mill and Deer Creeks

Gene Serr

When a survey party discovered Ishi and his hidden camp in rugged Deer Creek Canyon on November 5, 1908, they were surveying for a hydroelectric power project for the Oro Water, Light, and Power Company. When Thad Benner, James Savercool, and a few others moved into Mill Creek Canyon in the mid-1910s, a major reason was that they were offered stream gaging jobs with the Oro Company. What were Oro Water's plans for these remote canyons?

❧

The first hydroelectric power plants in the state were built in 1887, the first one near Colton in Southern California, and one near Grass Valley (1). Mill and Deer Creeks in Tehama County are inherently attractive for possible power development because of their relatively high summer flows and steep gradients. These sustained flows are because of their source in springs in lava country, which is also true of Battle Creek, Pit River, and North Fork Feather River. The latter streams are all highly developed for hydropower, whereas Mill and Deer Creeks have escaped such development, probably because of their smaller size and more remote location.

The earliest known hydropower proposal on Mill Creek was in 1900 when Douglas Cone (1867-1905) of Tehama County and Wayne Meredith, electrical engineer from San Francisco, announced a plan to "develop from 1,000 to 10,000 horsepower." Cone operated the large Cone Ranch, Cone Ice Company, and other interests after the death of his wealthy father, Joseph Cone, in 1894. This hydropower plan is known only from an optimistic but sketchy newspaper article, which included the statement that "a great part of this power will be directed to his [Cone's] personal interests, as he can apply it in many ways, and should a beet sugar factory be established near Tehama, power could be obtained for this." (2) Neither the sugar factory nor the power project ever materialized.

The earliest proposal known for Deer Creek was in 1901 when attorney Park Henshaw filed a water claim with the county for power purposes (3). Henshaw was president of the Butte County Electric Power and Lighting Company. (He was later one of four attorneys for Douglas Cone's estate.) The water claim location was deep in the canyon, a few miles below present Potato Patch Campground. The plan included a masonry diversion dam, a ditch and flume conveyance, a 36-inch pipe [penstock] and "water wheels" [power plant]. Henshaw was later a director of the Deer Creek Power Company, which filed incorporation papers in Tehama County in 1909 (4). Nothing further is known of this company.

The next proposal on Mill Creek is believed to be that of the Tehama County Power and Transportation Company in 1904. Surveyor Richard Gernon laid out a plan that started with a diversion dam at elevation 4,700, near the present Mill Creek Resort. (Gernon, 1850-1926, came to Red Bluff from Wisconsin in 1875, never married, and is buried at Oak Hill Cemetery.) An 8-mile conduit was proposed, finally dropping 1,200 feet in a penstock to a power plant. Two more diversion dams, conduits, and power plants were proposed downstream, the last plant being about 8 miles east of Tehama (5). Although it is not clear why this proposal died, it was probably related to the difficult access, high cost, and lack of funding.

The Oro Water, Light, and Power Company was formed in 1905 to consolidate several smaller companies serving water and power to Oroville, Thermalito, Palermo, and 18 gold dredges operating along the Feather River. The company also owned extensive gold-bearing gravel areas and five of the larger dredges. It operated three power plants on the West Branch of the Feather River with a transmission line to Oroville. It also owned

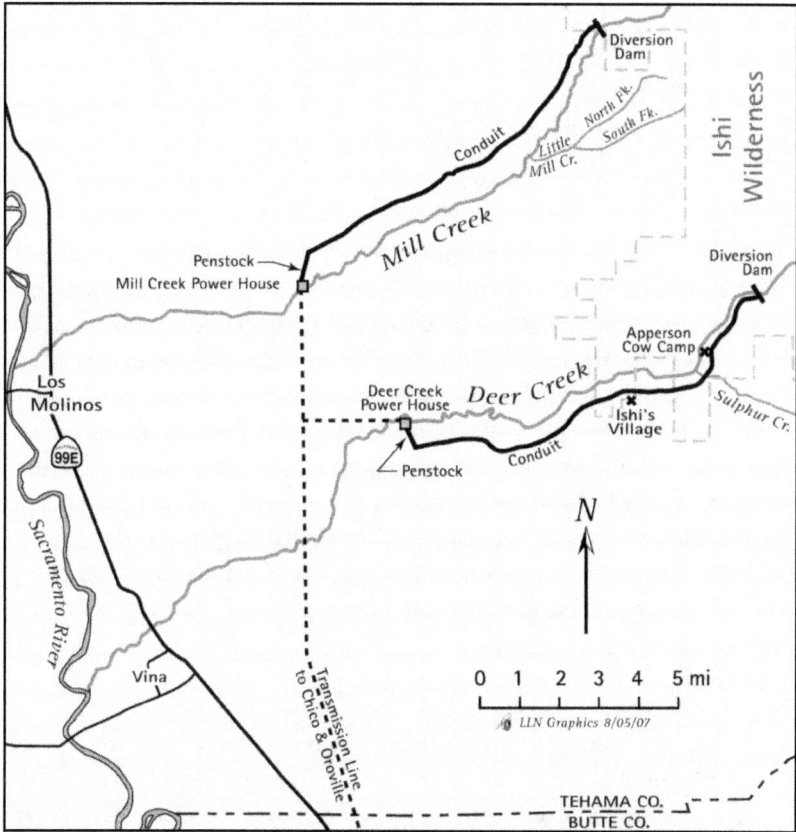

Map of Oro Water, Light & Power Company plan for hydropower development of Mill and Deer Creeks, 1910.

undeveloped property and water rights on Mill and Deer Creeks in Tehama County, and on several creeks in Plumas County.

In November 1908 Oro sent a crew of six engineers and surveyors into rugged Deer Creek Canyon to survey for a possible hydropower development. Their base camp was at Speegle's Sulphur Creek place, later called Apperson's Cow Camp, just upstream from the mouth of Sulphur Creek. The packers, guides, and hunters for the crew were J. M. "Jack" Apperson; his sons Albert, age 20, and Merle, 17; Charley Herrick; and Harry Keefer.

On November 5, young surveyors Ed Duensing and Al Lefferty were hiking in from Vina along Deer Creek with surveying gear to rejoin the crew. As they neared Sulphur Creek they came upon a near-naked Indian fishing with a spear. The Indian was Ishi, named later by anthropologist Alfred Kroeber. Both the surveyors and the Indian were startled and afraid, and parted quickly (6). Since the fascinating story of Ishi, the last of the Yahi, has been told many times, only the part with some relation to the Oro Company will be told in any detail here.

The next day guides Jack Apperson, Herrick, and Keefer returned to the spot where Ishi had been sighted and made a cautious search for Indians. In heavy brush about 400 feet above the creek they found the Indian camp, later called "Grizzly Bear's Hiding Place" by Theodora Kroeber. They saw two Indians flee up a cliff and found a sick old woman wrapped in a quilt stolen from the Speegle place. The guides proceeded to help themselves to the bows, arrows, fur-cape blankets, obsidian knives, and other stone and bone tools found. The following day, feeling some remorse at having taken all of the Indians' primitive means of survival, the party returned to give back the coveted trophies, along with a supply of food. However, the old woman and everything movable in the camp was gone, so the men kept the Indian material.

In 1910 Oro hired Galloway and Markwart, Civil Engineers of San Francisco, to recommend the best plan to develop power on their property in Tehama and Plumas counties. The consulting engineers found no good storage sites on Mill Creek and one questionable one on Deer Creek at Deer Creek Meadows. They indicated that the best development on both streams would involve diversion dams, conduits, penstocks, and power plants, with no storage. The recommended plan on Mill Creek involved a diversion dam about three miles above Little Mill Creek, 10.5 miles of conduit (part ditch, part flume) north of the creek, and a power plant about seven miles northeast of Los Molinos. The recommended plan on Deer Creek involved a diversion dam about two miles above Sulphur Creek, 10.5 miles of conduit south of the creek (combination of ditch, flume, and tunnel), and a power plant about eight miles east of Los Molinos (7, see map).

Two smaller power companies were also studying Mill Creek for power development about the same time—Butte and Tehama Power Company and Sierra Electric Power Company. However, their proposed developments were about ten miles upstream, entirely within Lassen National Forest. The engineer and founder of the Butte and Tehama company was Leon Bly (1877-1942) of Red Bluff, later to become controversial over the failed Bly

This is the only known photo of Leon Bly, who formed the Butte and Tehama Power Co. in 1909. He is shown here at Eagle Lake, about to sound the lake for his ill-fated Bly Tunnel project. Courtesy of Tim Purdy.

Tunnel at Eagle Lake. (Lingenfelter (8) lists him as a brother of the well-known Dr. Frederick Bly of Red Bluff, but Leon's obituary states that there were no known relatives.)

The Oro company became more interested in possible projects on Mill and Deer Creeks after receiving the report by Galloway and Markwart in 1910. They hired several settlers living along the creeks in 1914, including Thad Benner and James Savercool, to read staff gages (marked posts) set in the streams at different locations. The settlers were paid $35 per month to keep records in notebooks furnished by the company. Lorinda Hulseman, Benner's daughter, stated that she started helping keep the records as a young girl. She recalled reading gages twice a week at several locations on Mill Creek and once a week at Wilson Cove on Deer Creek (9). Periodically, engineers from Oro would make streamflow measurements at these gages to correlate with the gage height readings.

Mrs. Hulseman also mentioned that another family of settlers in Mill Creek canyon, the Kitchens, "were bootleggers who supplied the bigshots of the Oro Power Company with liquor" (9). (Actually they weren't "bootleggers" until Prohibition, 1920-33.) Considering the excellent fishing and hunting also available, the Oro officials and engineers probably managed to enjoy their pack trips into these remote canyons.

In 1911 Oro Water, Light, and Power Company became Oro Electric Corporation. Oro Electric acquired water rights and property along Mill and Deer Creeks, following the Galloway and Markwart plans, over the period 1911-16. The water rights were actually acquired from Galloway, who had posted claims to "15,000 miner's inches under 4-inch pressure" in each stream, witnessed by Markwart, early in 1911. This converts to 375 cfs (cubic feet per second). The engineers estimated the normal minimum summer flow in each stream at about 100 cfs.

Oro Electric soon got into a water rights dispute with the much larger Great Western Power Company, builders of Almanor Dam, over Butt Creek in Plumas County. Oro engineers built a diversion dam on Butt Creek, which the Great Western engineers blew up with dynamite. Court action continued from 1911 to 1917, when PG&E ended the fight by buying Oro Electric. In 1930 PG&E acquired Great Western in its final major consolidation, to become the first or second largest electric utility in the United States. This was the culmination of the gradual consolidation of over 400 small water and power companies in California over an 80-year period (1).

No further hydropower proposals for Mill or Deer Creeks are known until the 1980s. In 1978 a new federal law promoting hydropower development triggered a rush to develop small-scale plants throughout the state and country. The law required utilities such as PG&E to buy power at "avoided cost" rates, which meant rates equivalent to the price of foreign oil, or more than six cents a kilowatt-hour at that time. The law gave public entities such as Tehama County a "municipal preference" over private companies in developing power plants.

In 1981 the Tehama County Flood Control and Water Conservation District, under the leadership of County Supervisor Burt Bundy, was awarded a preliminary license by FERC (Federal Energy Regulatory Commission) for a three-part power project on Mill Creek. Three private proposals were turned down. The county proposal included three separate diversions and power plants with a total length of about 34 miles (10). The plan was similar to Gernon's proposal back in 1904. The county also had proposals on South Fork Battle Creek, which appeared more favorable than the one on Mill Creek. The county would probably have made an agreement with a private company for construction and operation of the project, then sold the power to PG&E and used the revenue to fund local government and infrastructure. However, PG&E finally claimed it did not have the transmission capacity needed, which largely ended the county's interest in possible hydropower revenue.

Only one small hydropower project was ever built on Mill or Deer Creeks. In 1980 the Fire Mountain Lodge Hydroelectric Project was built on a tributary to Gurnsey Creek at Fern Springs in the Deer Creek drainage, about a half mile east of the Fire Mountain Lodge complex, by the owner of the lodge, Ken Willis. It consists of a 6-foot-high and 30-foot-long concrete and rockfill dam impounding water from a collection of springs, a 1,540-foot penstock, and a 45-horsepower Pelton wheel turbine. The operating capacity is only 15 kW due to flow and head limitations at the site (11).

With the creation of the 41,000-acre Ishi Wilderness Area, including portions of Mill and Deer Creeks, in 1984, the chances of any further hydropower proposals of significant size on these streams became highly unlikely. An even more important factor is the ongoing joint effort by several state and federal agencies to reestablish significant salmon runs on these creeks and on Battle Creek. (Five of the diversion dams on Battle Creek and tributaries are planned for removal in cooperation with PG&E.) It is interesting that the discovery of Ishi fishing for salmon on Deer Creek by a power project survey crew in 1908 eventually resulted in the protection of Mill and Deer Creeks from such development, probably for all time.

Sources

1. Coleman, Charles M. 1952. *P. G. and E. of California.*

2. *Red Bluff Daily News,* Jan. 12, 1900.

3. *Red Bluff Daily News,* Oct. 2, 1901.

4. Red Bluff Evening Sentinel, Dec. 21, 1909.

5. *Red Bluff Daily News,* June 23, 1904.

6. Burrill, Richard. 2001. *Ishi Rediscovered.*

7. Galloway and Markwart. 1910. "Report of the Properties of Oro, Water, Light, and Power Company."

8. Lingenfelter, Keith. 1996. Tehama County Pioneers, 1996,

9. Mill Creek Conservancy. 1997. *Mill Creek Watershed Management Strategy Report,* App. G.

10. *Red Bluff Daily News,* Dec. 14, 1981, 4:1.

11. Federal Register, June 1, 2005, Vol. 70, No. 104, Notices.

Tales From Ishi Country (available at TehamaCountyHistory.com)

Deer Creek Canyon near the Mt. Diablo meridian. It's 800 feet to the creek from the camera, c. 1911.

Office tent, c. 1911

1911 Deer Creek Water Survey

A few years ago, photos documenting a survey by the San Francisco civil engineering firm of Galloway & Markwart were generously donated to the Society. For two years, this firm had been looking into the feasibility of building a hydropower plant at the junction of Sulphur and Deer Creeks, 18 miles east of Vina. These photos document the March-June 1911 survey into Deer Creek Canyon, which is mentioned in the preceding story.

☙

One of the members of this survey crew was Frank S.M. Harris who wrote an article for the San Francisco Call *in June 1911, portions of which are excerpted here to accompany the photos from the album.*

In A California Canyon Hides the Last Wild Indians of America
Frank S.M. Harris

Deer Creek is a wild territory. Upon its rocky slopes flourish only the live oak and the buckeye, intermingled with thickets of deer brush and poison oak. Fires have raged over large areas of manzanita growth, leaving their main trunks standing black and desolate. Cliff upon cliff tower above the stream bottom, at times sheer walls. At intervals along the main canyon, tributary arroyos enter, smaller examples of the same rugged topography.

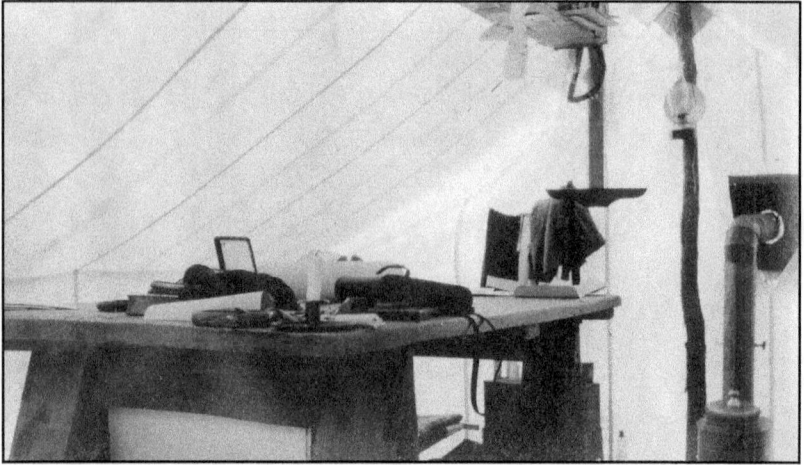

Interior of office tent.

Part of camp at Speegle's.

Part of camp at Speegle's.

Speegle's cabin at Sulphur Creek.

Sulphur Creek after a violent storm.

Sunday morning.

Great masses of conglomerate have detached themselves in ages past from the main cliff and have shattered upon the cliffs beneath. Sharp crags and pinnacles of more resistant materials stand out against the sky line. It is a territory that is seldom visited by man, for there is no reason for his coming and many an excuse for his remaining elsewhere. On the whole, it is the ideal habitat for a race of wild men, satisfying even the most fastidious in scenic effects.

I found myself by the side of a campfire in the very heart of the Deer Creek country. On one side of me sat a civil engineer; on the other side a professional hunter for Deer Creek is the home of the lion and panther and the bounty of each makes hunting a profitable sport. Opposite were a couple of cattlemen and another engineer. Collegian talked with cow puncher and cow puncher with collegian for there are no distinctions, mental, moral, or physical, "in the brush." The conversation was general in the extreme, drifting from stray horses to the height of the grass on the ranges; and from the winnings at a Piute game to the cost of rifle shells. At last, the Nozis were mentioned, and it was then that I heard at first had hand the story of their discovery, for to these men belongs the credit of unearthing all that remains of this lost tribe.

A party of these engineers had penetrated far into the interior of Deer Creek canyon in search of a possible water power [1908]. With the greatest difficulty, they had finally carried their lines through almost impenetrable brush and over well nigh vertical cliffs to a point near the spot where we sat. They had only been camped there a short time when articles from their outfit began to disappear. It would have been an easy matter for a person to raid the tents, as all members of the part were absent from camp during the greater portion of the day. But to the best of their knowledge, there were no others in that part of the canyon. Suspicion naturally fell upon some animal. The mess tent in particular was subject to inroad, the principal loss consisting of several cans of lard. This led the campers to conclude that an animal could not be the robber since the pails of lard were tightly sealed and cased. These events continued for several days, culminating in the theft of a rifle.

On the day following the loss of the rifle, one of their number a boy of 18, the "water buck" for the party, chanced to be in advance of the others, when without the least warning, he came upon an Indian on a rock in the middle of the stream spearing a fish. The Indian is said to have motioned the boy away, a command which was complied with on the part of the boy

A quiet game.

John Apperson standing by a makeshift Yahi Indian camp dwelling on Deer Creek, which was discovered by the 1908 survey crew (private collection).

Survey crew (no names).

Looking up Sulphur Creek.

Deer Creek Canyon north from Speegle's.

Remains of old cabin.

Cliffs west of Speegle's. Highest point on extreme left is 500 feet; average is 300 feet.

Acorn Hollow,

At Dave Robert's place.

Sacramento Valley from Tehama County foothills.

Crossing the creek at Graham's.

Looking up Deer Creek from just below Pine Creek. Pine Creek comes down between two hills on right.

Frank S. M. Harris (author of newspaper article quoted in this article) at Deer Creek gaging station.

Pack train.

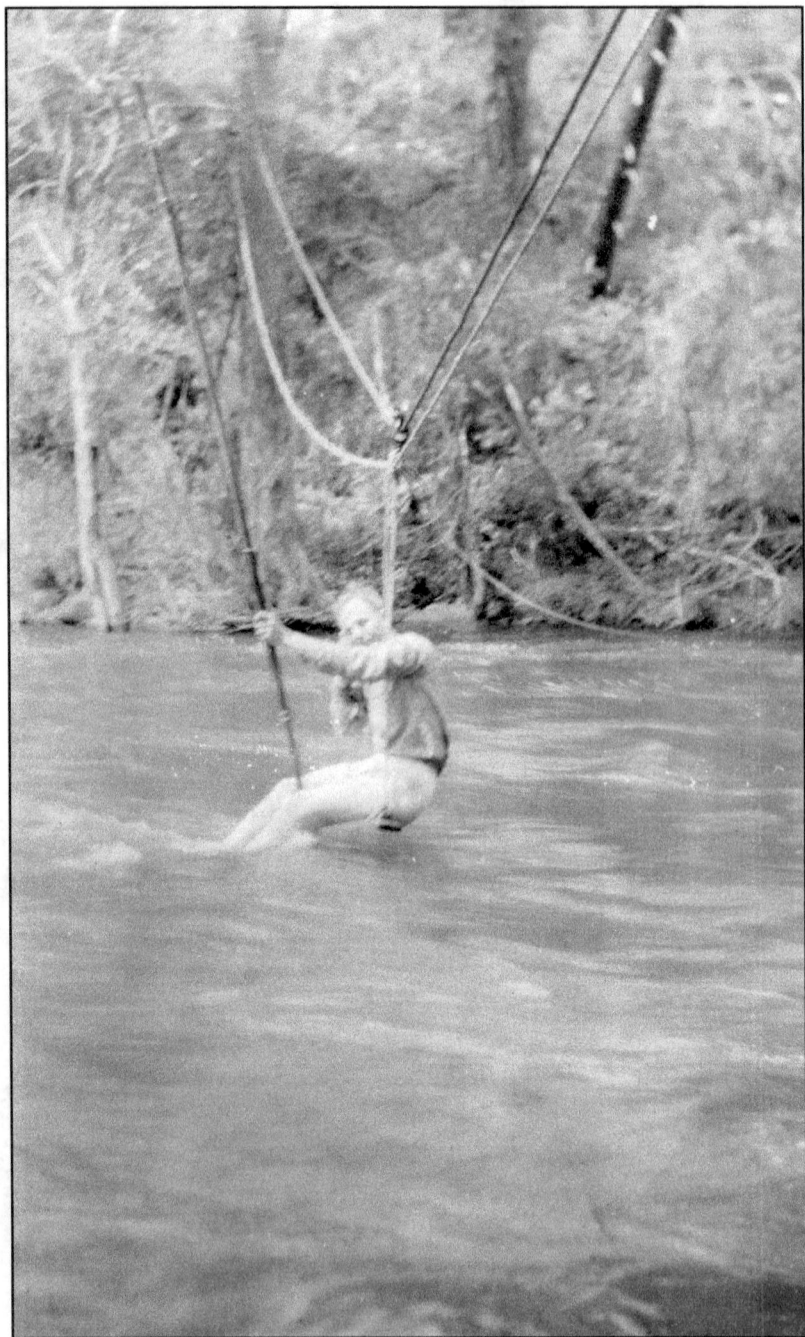

Erle Long Cope gaging over Deer Creek—862 sec.ft flowing.

Chimney Rock, 250 feet high (between the ears).

Transit party near end of work.

Camp at Graham's cabin.

Leaving camp.

Acorn Hollow camp.

Near Pine Creek.

with considerable alacrity. He, with the others, returned to the scene of the encounter, but could find not the slightest clue, even in the soft beds of the river sand, of the direction taken by the man.

It was then late in the afternoon and the chase had to be abandoned for the day.

On the following two days, the entire surveying party, together with several packers and cattlemen, engaged in a diligent search of the vicinity. At last, when nearly discouraged by the impenetrable brush and the huge boulders, Jack Apperson by name, chanced upon a slight indication of a trail through the scrub oak. No track was to be seen underfoot because of the rock covering the surface, but the boughs has been displaced and here and there a small limb had snapped. Crawling on hands and knees for a distance of 100 yards further, the explorers came upon the encampment, or rather where the encampment had been, for the Indians had departed but a few hours before. All had not gone, however.

In the center of the camp sat an old woman. At the approach of the White men, she made a last attempt to creep away into the thicket but sank back in exhaustion. Apperson offered her a canteen. She made signs to inquire what it contained, and upon being assured that it was water, drank nearly all of it. The men then asked her if she had any papooses. Catching the word "papoose" she groaned and, extending her arms with a sweeping motion, shook her head to indicate that they were scattered.

The camp stood on a steep hillside along the upper end of which were erected huts. Small poles of pine had been thrust into the slope and extended some eight or ten feet nearly horizontally. These were bound to an arch-like frame on the front. Over these poles were spread deerskins and fragments of grain sacks purloined from time to time from campers. Next above the skins had been placed a layer of earth several inches in thickness, covered in turn by carefully laid twigs, pine needles, and ferns. To a person approaching these habitations from the uphill side, it gave the appearance of a mass of debris such as accumulates behind a fallen log on a steep slope. In fact, they are indiscernible at a distance of thirty feet. There were several of these huts used for sleeping quarters and for storing food.

Upon entering, it was found to contain innumerable articles. There were locks of guns broken to pieces, indicating that the Indians had no idea of their use. Pieces of pottery were in abundance, but from their positions

Dave Roberts, Jack Glackin (sp?), and Jess Cope.

Deer Creek at Speegle's.

about the enclosure, it was decided that their function was one of ornament rather than utility. Under another bit of shelter stood the cans of lard, which the engineers had lost but a few says before. The Indians, after opening the cans, had thrust their fingers into the lard to sample its flavor, but had not thought of using it for cooking purposes.

In one corning of the encampment was a pot of acorns, the water in which was but slightly below the boiling temperature, yet search as they might, they White men could find no trace of the fire, so successfully had it been concealed lest the smoke betray their whereabouts.

A trail led down to the creek from which the water supply was obtained. The brush was carefully interwoven to form a low arched passage through which one could walk only when bent over. Even here no footprints were in evidence, except where some rotted wood had been pulverized. At one point, this creek trail dropped over a steep descent; so steep that it became necessary to grasp the surrounding trees for support.

One particular feature of the camp that cannot be explained is the small stone mounds that have been heaped up in the very center of the opening. At the time of the first entry, there were none of these; but some three months later, upon returning, five were found. At present they number 11. Nothing is buried beneath them. ◎

Charles S. Avery (1838-1915) and the cabin he built in Mill Creek Canyon about 1880. Photo taken in 1914 (Tehama County Library archives).

The Hermit of Mill Creek Canyon

Anderson Finley
(Red Bluff Sentinel, January 17, 1934)

About the year 1869 a man by the name of John M. [L.?] Boles (1) took up a homestead in Mill Creek canyon about a half mile above Black Rock, which stands on the south side of the creek, about fifty miles from its mouth. He was a bachelor about 50 years old, stood six feet four or five inches high, straight as an arrow, and weighed 200 pounds. He had plenty of black whiskers, blue eyes, a hand like a bear's paw, and a foot like a ham. He was well educated, an interesting talker, and at one time a representative from one of the northern counties to the state legislature of California. He was the first white man to make a home in the Mill Creek canyon country. He built a large hewn-log house with stone fireplace, planted a vineyard, and set out several varieties of fruit trees which he brought in, together with his supplies, over a rugged trail on pack animals. There were lots of game of all kinds and plenty of trout in the stream nearby. He had a garden, some chickens, a dog, and a few cows.

Such was J.M. Boles and his surroundings. When I first met him in 1874, his latch string always hung on the outside of his door, and a note inviting "eat all you want and please wash the dishes." This man was sitting of top of the world, so to speak, happy, contented, and monarch of all he surveyed. He took a great liking to me; often asked me to visit him, and quite frequently I did. He told me of losing his mother when he was a small lad, of his ambition to become a great lawyer, his education cut short before he had finished college. [He also told of] his wanderings in Mexico and his landing in California during the gold rush, his association with the tough high and the low and the tender elements of those days, and of the final determination to get away from the hubbub of struggling humanity and become a hermit. He said Mill Creek Canyon furnished most everything he needed, and he was happy

When he first came there, bears gave him a lot of trouble. They kept killing his hogs, 'til he had to give up that part of his industry. But he concluded to make hogs out of bears. There was plenty of them, and they were really fat at hog-killing time. Why raise hogs when bears would furnish juicy hams and plenty of grease for his venison, and nice rugs for his floors? He went to Vina and had a blacksmith make a double-spring steel trap that weighed 42 pounds. This solved his hog problem. He afterwards gave this trap to Charles Avery, Sr., who at one time Mr. Boles tried to kill. I will tell of this later.

About 1877 Boles sold his place and cattle to two brothers, Dave and Sandy Archibald (2). He then located at Bucks Flat, which lies on a high promontory between the middle and south forks of Antelope Creek and is surrounded by rim rocks on three sides (3). Here he planted another orchard, built a comfortable home, and spent his declining years. It was here that I met C.S. Avery, Sr., that prince of the mountains, whom nobody knew but to love (4). In my mind his name shines like a diamond scroll. We spent many happy days together, and I knew Charley Avery. He was a stationary engineer. Howard and Kraft built a sawmill at Howard Meadows in 1869 (5), and later Avery ran the engine for them. In the winter time there was not much doing, and Charley put in part of his time hunting and trapping in Mill Creek canyon, and a part of it with Mr. Boles when he lived there.

One morning they started on a hunt together with the understanding that they meet at a pine flat a mile or so ahead, which both were acquainted with. Charley got there first, killed a deer, and was on his knees in the act of dressing it when he heard a shot; and he knew someone had taken a crack at him. He saw Boles standing about a hundred yards away, but could not believe he had done the shooting. However, when Boles came within speaking distance, Charley knew from his actions and looks [that] he was the hombre, and asked him what he was shooting at. He was shaking like a leaf and white as a ghost, but managed to say: "Charley, I shot at you thinking you was a bear." Charley told me he thought at the time that Boles was "crazy." He told him to march ahead towards home, leaving the deer where it was. Charley said by the time they got back to the ranch, they had both got over their scare, and he was satisfied it was willful carelessness on Boles' part. The next morning they went back and got the deer they had left. But always after that they hunted in opposite directions.

About the year 1876, Chris Kauffman, one of a family of early Tehama County pioneers (6), located a quartz claim some 7 or 8 miles above Black Rock in Mill Creek canyon. He, with Dr. Cameron and Dr. Olendorf (leading lights of Red Bluff at that time), formed a company and commenced the development of Kauffman's prospect, which he called the Sooner mine. It contained a great deal of chloride of expectations and sulphides of disappointment, and after a year or so they gave it up.

During the seventies and early eighties, I was working on the flume for the Sierra Lumber Company and generally put in the winter months on repair work. But in the winter of '81 and '82 I decided to take a lay off and have some sport hunting and trapping. With my old friend Charley Avery we picked on the old Sooner mine for our playground. There was plenty of bear and deer in that rough country and plenty of trout in the creek nearby and no game laws. Oh boy, this was the life. One of my ancestors, John Finley, was a companion of Daniel Boone in the early days of Kentucky, and I think one of his bugs of adventure was with me then and is still going strong.

We took in a good supply of provisions, reading matter, tobacco, two new Winchesters and ammunition, two bear traps, including the Boles trap and several smaller ones. We repaired the old cabin, made a mattress of cedar boughs, built a smoke house; and with Cub and Crowder, our two dogs, we were fixed. We soon had juicy venison and a big fat bear, which furnished plenty of lard for our cooking. Charley tried his hand at making bear bacon and curing hams, but it was all forbear for me. Our extra meat we salted and hung in our smoke house, and by spring we had a lot of dried venison, hams, and jerky.

When not hunting we put in the time dressing skins and exploring. On the south side of the canyon about a mile above camp we discovered a great many caves, where numerous Indians had made their homes at one time. One of these was extra large, with two chambers above. The means of access was by a kind of ladder made from a tree about 20 feet long with the stubs of the limbs for steps. This makeshift had stood there so long it had a metallic ring when struck with an ax. We took a lot of pleasure in decorating ourselves like the frontier men of old. We made moccasins which we wore all winter; and our wild-cat skin caps, with the ears in front and the tails behind, must have looked the part at least.

On the whole we had a most enjoyable winter. With a companion like Charley Avery one could not get out of sorts or be lonesome. He was a brawny fellow and could shoulder a large buck and carry him to camp with little effort.

In 1882 Avery married Ellen Wilson [Hunley?] and located a homestead near the junction of Boat Gunnel Hollow and Mill Creek where he lived with his son, young Charley as he was called for many years. They were interested in the cattle business. Charley Avery loved the mountains and wide open spaces. He passed over the Great Divide in 1903 and rests by the side of his old friend, Adolph Olsen, in the Red Bluff cemetery (7). ◉

Charles E. Avery (1882-1963), son of Charles S. Avery and a respected cattleman (TCGHS archives).

Sources

1. John Lucas Boles (1825-1893)—Born in Ohio, never married, died intestate in Red Bluff with no heirs. He appeared in the 1860 Sierra District census as a farmer and miner. (Lingenfelter, *Tehama County Pioneers*, 1989, available at TehamaCountyHistory.com)

2. David Archibald (1845-?)—Born in Nova Scotia, and married Sarah Hoag in Tehama County in 1879. Farmer and stockman at Yellow Jacket (Howard Meadows) in 1884.

Alexander (Sandy) Archibald—Born in Nova Scotia, married Susan Gist, in Tehama County, 1884. Laborer and stockman at Champion Mill in 1883. (From Hitchcock, *Leaves of the Past*, 1980 [microfilm])

3. Bucks Flat—See article "Tales from Bucks Flat," in this collection.

4. Charles Stanton Avery (1838-1915)—Born in Connecticut, and came to California in 1861. Married Ellen Hunley, Tehama County, in 1881. Lumberman at Champion Mill in 1910. (Hitchcock)

5. Howard Meadows is about three miles southeast of old Lyonsville (Champion Mill). Named for Daniel Howard (1826-?), who built and operated the old (1868) and new (1877) Yellow Jacket mills there. The mills were shut down in 1881. (Hitchcock)

6. Christopher Kauffman (1835-1887)—Born Pennsylvania. Operated a store at Belle Mill, 1872, (Hitchcock) Prior to the Sooner mine failure, Kauffman had worked another mining claim near Boatgunnel Hill, about six miles below Black Rock, which was also a failure.

7. Adolph Olsen (1851-1919)—Born in Sweden. Married Alice Shelton, Tehama County, 1886. Listed as a Finley Lake stockman in 1910. (Hitchcock)

❧

Anderson Finley (1859-1937) moved to the Belle Mill Road area of Tehama County with his parents from Milpitas in 1871, when he was 12 years old. Finley Lake and Finley Butte are named for his father, William Finley, who had come to California with the Evans emigrant train in 1852. Anderson became a telegraph operator for the Sierra Lumber Company at Finley Lake about 1880. Although he married and moved to Oregon in 1889, in his later years he visited in Tehama County and wrote a series of articles on the "good old days" of his youth.

The fact that the annual "rootin' tootin' Wild West roundup had to be put on hold due to the absences of so many young men serving their country, did not prevent the Naval Ferry Command from entering a float in what may have been the celebration of VE Day on May 13, 1945.

Cowboys and Sailors

Arla Gridley Farmer

For the last two years of WWII, Red Bluff, California, was transformed by the presence of the Naval Air Transport Command Ferry Service Unit, FSU-9.

Red Bluff became a stopping point for planes being ferried from the East Coast to the Pacific with a regular contingent of Naval aviators and support staff stationed there. Many of the members of FSU-9 settled in Red Bluff and other Northern California towns after the war and the many ways they contributed to their new communities. Names include Clarence "Boots" Batson (he taught at Bidwell School and was principal at Lincoln School in Red Bluff), Thomas W. Walker (Walker Lithograph); Harold Emery, Joe Dougherty, and Arnold "Duke" Stelling.

The arrival of FSU-9 has had unexpected and profound effects on this community for the last fifty-five years. Whether you are a WWII buff, love military history or flying, are a native of Northern California, or just love stories about real people, this book should be added to your library. Former Dairyville resident Arla Farmer chronicled those WWII days when rationing was the rule and old-fashioned ingenuity kept life interesting for the men of FSU-9. This book tells that story.

Through a generous donation from Arla's family (thank you Dee Linton!!), the Society now has copies of this previously out-of-print book for sale on our website (yehamacountyhistory.com). Proceeds from all our books help support the Society's mission to preserve the history of Tehama County and legacies such as Arla Farmer's. Additionally, we will donate a portion of each sale of this book to the Charles Krause Aviation Museum whose volunteers are working hard to set it up again after losing their space at the airport. We risk losing that incredible aviation history if nothing is done. The Tehama County Genealogical & Historical Society is committed to help so this history can be seen and enjoyed. Here is an excerpt from the book for your enjoyment. ◎

> Aviation mechanic Jack Dorsey was from Omaha, Nebraska and far from a "bruiser." He was at the Blue Ribbon bar one night with two friends when several cowboys came in. One of them, taking in the three men in uniform, threw down the glove with, "Where's the water? No ships around here." Jack immediately took umbrage, one word led to another, and Jack found himself tossed behind the bar. Outraged, he climbed back out, ready to do battle, but was promptly thrown back again.
>
> Peering over the bar, the assailants regarded each other in dead silence. "Well come on," urged one of the cowboys.
>
> "You big lug. If you think I'm coming out from behind this bar, you're crazy," Jack responded.
>
> Everyone laughed. "I'm buying you a drink," offered the cowboy, ending the confrontation.

The Moritz Thomsen house with detail of the "naked lady" mosaic bathtub. Photos from Tehama County Assessor's office (house) and J. Woods (bathtub).

Moritz Thomsen and the Naked Lady of Vina

Josie Reifschneider-Smith

About 10 years ago, the Society received an inquiry about the Moritz Thomsen house somewhere near Vina. I knew exactly who to ask about it— long-time Vina resident Frances Leininger. Before I finished telling her the name, she said,

"Moritz! I knew him well. We grew watermelons near his house. He was good friends with my brother Albert. Moritz raised hogs that he'd sell to Minch in Red Bluff, but he'd let them run in that house too. Then there was the naked lady in the bathroom that was very popular with the men."

Wait! What?

Moritz Thomsen, III, c. 1920s (Museum of History and Industry, Seattle, WA).

Before we get into that, let me tell you a little bit about Martin Moritz Thomsen Titus. He came from a very wealthy family from Seattle—his grandfather (and namesake) was a wealthy businessman and his father was president of Centennial Mills (Krusteaz brand of flours). His mother, Elvera Anderson Thomsen was a photographer and began her career managing Edward Curtis's studio (Curtis is famous for his Native American photography). However, family dynamics (he and his father, whom he described as tyrannical, never got along) made him determined to make his own way in life. After WWII, where he had served in Europe as a B-17 bombardier for the U.S. Eighth Air Force, Moritz found his way to Tehama County where he became a farmer by day and a writer by night. He did pretty well until outside factors, including the demand for leaner pork, caused prices to decline to the point that he was forced to sell out. With no other options left, he decided to join the recently formed Peace Corps after seeing a commercial about it on television. At 50, he wasn't sure if he would qualify, but he was accepted and sent to Ecuador (1965-1967). While Moritz likened the Peace Corp as an exercise in "intellectual exploration" and perhaps "the last great adventure available to Americans," his father "disowned him as a Communist radical."

After the Peace Corps, Moritz remained in Ecuador where he died of cholera in 1991 at the age of 76. Always been a writer, he published several books about his adventures while in Ecuador. In fact, his first book, *Living Poor*, is considered the best book about the Peace Corps experience ever written. He even wrote articles for the *Red Bluff Daily News* that were published in 1966 and 1967 under the column "Ambassador in Levis."

But what about his house? Research shows that it was designed by renowned San Francisco architect Mario Corbett and built by Heininger & Stover of Corning in 1950. It was on Moritz's 300-acre alfalfa farm (called "Cowpie Ranch") near the Sacramento River (east side) and just south of present-day Woodson Bridge Recreation Area. It was two levels and faced east. The entire eastern side was one large 15-foot tall screened-in porch complete with indoor garden. Inside, large sliding glass panels acted as doors or walls that could be opened to take advantage of the fresh air and provide an open concept within the house. Built of redwood, cork, pine, plywood, and river rock, it cost $16,000 to build. It won an award

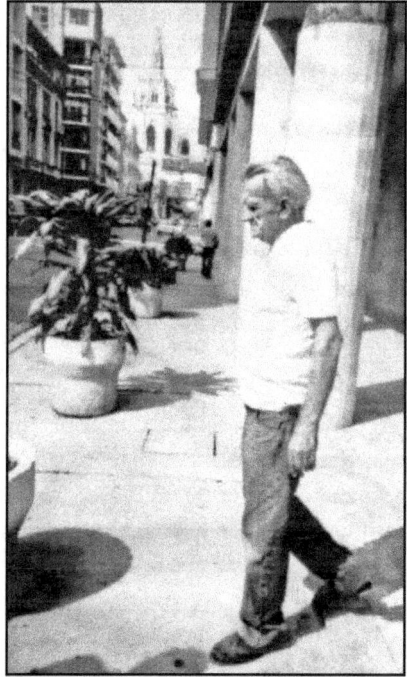

Moritz Thomsen, Guayaquil, Ecuador, 1990 (CC-BY-SA-3.0, Valentinaavbc).

from the American Institute of Architects in 1952. Photos published in magazines and books of the time show a very neat and lovely mid-century modernist home—not a hog in sight.

Now about that bathroom. The July 1952 issue of *The Magazine of Building* notes that George Albert Harris (1913-1991) designed a mosaic tub to be a "colorful [and] integral work of art."[1] George was not only Moritz's brother-

---

1 Harris was a painter, muralist, and printmaker. Born in San Francisco, he studied art at the California School of Fine Arts. In 1934, he was accepted into the WPA Federal Art Project and was one of the youngest artists on the mural project at Coit Tower. Harris taught at San Francisco State College, San Francisco Museum of Modern Art, Stanford University, and the California College of Arts and Crafts. He obtained his Ph.D. from Stanford and taught at Notre Dame College in Belmont, California, Emanuel College in Boston, and Sussex, England. He moved to southern France where he painted until his death. George Harris was a member of the San Francisco Art Association and the American Artists Congress. His works are represented in the San Francisco Museum of Modern Art, the Library of Congress, and the National Gallery of Art in Washington, D.C. (annexgalleries.com/artists/biography/960/Harris/George).

in-law but a noted artist who painted murals at Coit Tower ("Banking and the Law") and the Chamber of Commerce in San Francisco and whose art is housed in many prominent museum collections. Tehama County was graced with a notable piece of his art—the "naked lady" bathtub—that made instant art connoisseurs out of many local men.

So where is this house that has such a remarkable history attached to it? Sadly, it fell into disrepair and was torn down sometime in the 2000s. A walnut orchard stands where it once did, and the "naked lady" is no more.

Hog Farming in Tehama County and the Peace Corps In His Own Words[2]

By the end of 1964 I was probably the largest producer of fat hogs in Northern California; hell, I was probably the only hog producer in Northern California. In those years it cost eighteen cents a pound to produce a market hog. The price fell to sixteen, to fourteen, to twelve cents a pound. It stayed at twelve cents for months. I was losing about twelve dollars on every hog I sold and selling about twelve hundred a year. I was almost the last of the World War II veterans who had gone into farming in 1945 and was still operating almost twenty years later; everyone, all my friends, had given up in despair. They had faded away with dignity, after all they had children to feed, but I felt much luckier than them. I can't remember now why I didn't fade away with dignity; I think it simply never occurred to me that I should do anything besides farm or that, with the sacrifices I was prepared to make, somehow, I wouldn't be allowed to do it.

To hell with dignity. During the last few months, I didn't own a pair of Levis that didn't have butter-plate-sized holes at the knees and at the ass. I lost my house and twenty acres of pasture where I ran the dry sows, and moved onto the property where I had built the farrowing pens in the middle of a pretty, abandoned olive orchard. There was no house on this land so I put a bed and a table in a little tool shed and installed the stove and the refrigerator in one of the farrowing pens; it wasn't too bad except on the coldest days, but it didn't take long to heat up a can of hash, which is what I virtually lived on one winter. After it was all over, on the day that I arrived in Montana to begin Peace Corps training, I had $23 in my pocket; this represented all my capital, everything that I had accumulated in twenty years as a California farmer.

---

2 Compiled from *The Farm on the River of Emeralds* and *Red Bluff Daily News*, June 22, 1944.

There are certain days in life so packed with horror or revelation that if you survive them, your whole past stands rendered, the essence so distilled and clarified that it is impossible to keep on deluding yourself. In the revelation department one thinks of those religious conversions that strike one down like lightning, turning drunkards or thieves into missionaries. Days of revelation are the mileposts in life. But in the horror department, I have been remembering a couple of those days now. They are separated by years, but each helps to explain how, at some 50 years of age, I ended up on a jungle farm [in Ecuador]. If it was twenty years of farming in California that almost killed me, it was [Ecuador] that brought me back to life.

Early morning in California on a day in April of 1965. I was out in the farrowing house making coffee. It was chilly, and I was planning to take the coffee and crouch under one of the heat lamps with a bunch of newly hatched pigs when there was a furious skidding of wheels on gravel and my neighbor drove into the yard and began screaming at me. My dogs had been chasing his sheep again. He had warned me three times and he swore to God that the next time he would arrive with the sheriff and a warrant for my arrest.

Oh God. The dogs had been a real problem; there were six of them—the mother, Langendorf, and her five pups. I had spent months trying to give them away, without success. One afternoon I took all the dogs into the Vina grocery store and stayed there until closing time, begging anyone who came in to take a dog home. One of my friends, Marie, took one out of pity, but brought it back to me three days later because her other dog, a truly ancient and overfed spayed bitch, was neurotically jealous of the new dog. There was nothing special about that pack of dogs: they were sturdy country types with country manners who tried desperately to ingratiate themselves by leaping and licking. They had long noble tails like pampas grass. They ran all over the dry hills between Vina and Corning, and if they saw a bunch of sheep grazing on those worthless acres, they would rush down to play with them. They were not killers; they were lovers. At night they would all crowd into the toolshed where I lay on the bed watching TV, and sleep underneath the table. And slowly, very sneakily, one by one they would creep up onto the bed with me so that in the morning I would be all but crushed by their weight or blown out through the door by all those wildly thrashing tails.

I had a young cat, too, who slept with me, always the same way, stretching her whole length out on my chest and putting her face as close to mine as she could. The cat and I were very close, very tender with one another. Aside from the six dogs, the cat, and about nine hundred and fifty pigs, I had very little contact with the world. I had become an embarrassment to the farm community as my assets faded away and my lifestyle turned brutal and ascetic; I was no longer an advertisement for the free enterprise system.

Until that day, the destruction had scarcely touched me. But now that day had arrived, and now it was time to make another sacrifice, one so terrible that I had never imagined it and never prepared myself. I was about to be put in jail as a public menace to the United States sheep industry, and I was going to have to kill my dogs. I went out into the fattening pens and filled a couple of feeders, noticing that almost all the hog feed was gone and that I had to call the feed mill and tell them to get on the ball. I washed down the hog pens that were beginning to receive the sun, separated a couple of droopy pigs into the hospital area, and fed the sows in the farrowing house. Moisture condensing on the ratters had dripped down and burnt out a couple of the heat lamps; I replaced them. I went into the last farrowing pen, the kitchen, and drank more coffee, squatting outside in the sun in the gutter and looking into the branches of the olive trees, their leaves silver and glistening on this spring morning. It hadn't occurred to me, not once, that two months from now this whole place would be nailed up and deserted. When finally it was absolutely time to go, I walked down to the truck and sat behind the wheel with the door open, and the dogs, watching me and knowing that the open door meant that they were going for a ride, rushed into the front seat delirious with joy. They had never traveled all together like this and they were all half-crazy with excitement, all of them fighting to stick their noses out through the partly opened windows.

After I had dropped off my dogs at the pound, I drove on to Red Bluff and the slaughterhouse. A day before, I had sold forty fat hogs, and while Mr. Minch liked a couple of days' notice, I had decided out of necessity to harass him for the money. I was a hog man, and he knew that I was going down the drain, and it was very seldom that he was blatantly rude to me when I arrived a day early looking for money. But first I called the feed mill in Ord Bend about my empty feed bins. I was immediately put through to the owner who quite politely informed me that since I had a $4,000 feed bill, and with the new drop in hog prices, it seemed extremely unlikely that I could pay this obligation; the mill could send me no more feed on credit. It was stunning news, or rather, ordinarily it would have been stunning news to learn that I was being closed down, but I was already so numbed by the loss of my dogs that I could scarcely take it in. I continued on to the slaughterhouse. Mr. Minch, about six months away from the heart attack that would kill him, was rushing around in his office keeping everything going. He was provoked that I had not had the decency to wait another day but promised to make me out a check. "It's going to take a few minutes, though," he said. "While you're waiting, why don't you go out in the cooling room and look at your hogs. I'm sorry I can't give you top price, but they have way too much back fat. I'm going to have to dock you."

I had never seen my pigs after they had been killed, and looking at them then—all strung up on iron hooks, split down the middle, as pink and smooth as babies, hanging in a long row in the semidarkness—it was hard to imagine them snuffling around my feet in the fattening pens and twirling and dancing with delight under the jet of water I used to play on them during the heat of the afternoons. Out of the hundreds that I had, there were a few with whom I have had rather friendly relations. We liked one another; we teased one another; they regarded me as an equal, and it was important to them to be touched and talked to and to be recognized. In the evenings while they rested, I used to play Shostakovich symphonies for them. I really did not want to look at my pigs with their lousy extra tenth of an inch of back fat, lined up and still and unbelievably dead in that dark cement room. Beginning to stagger just a little, beginning to pant just a little, I left by the closest door into another cement room, but one that was flooded with sunlight and crowded with men in white coats who were furiously cutting and hacking at the carcasses of cows.

No one will ever convince me that all this was simply coincidence and that four-hour period was not organized and orchestrated to bring me crashing down. I had fallen under the malevolent eye of God, and He had more tricks up his sleeve. I didn't know if I could take any more that day, but I remember thinking, "It's coming, whether or not you can take anymore, and it's coming today," and the idea flashed through my head that by nine o'clock that night someone would come to the farm with a telegram announcing the death of someone that I loved and couldn't lose. But nothing that violent was needed now; all I needed was one more light tap on the head. It came in the next ten seconds.

I was going into deep shock, the blood vessels in my limbs so constricted that the blood felt like thickening honey; my hands and feet were ice, and in the fuse box of my head the connections were going dead or grounding out, and pinwheels of daring light like strobes whirled and sputtered. Staggering, paralyzed, reeling as though I was losing my balance, I put out my hand to steady myself on the flank of an immense and placid cow who was standing at my side. As I touched her there was the crack of a rifle in my ear, and the cow dropped at my feet. In that space that a moment before she had occupied, standing on a little raised platform like a podium, was the largest Negro I have ever seen. He was bare to the waist and glistening with sweat, and he was looking deep into my face and laughing at me. A cold little thread of smoke rose from the gun he was holding.

I had an old television set in my shack, which I had bought secondhand for fifteen dollars. That night the cat and I lay on the bed watching it. It was April but tonight it was icy cold in the shack, even under the covers. Sometime that evening, I watched a minute-long spot advertisement for the Peace Corps. Their propaganda at that time was in one of its tell-it-as-it-is phases, and we lay there watching a young volunteer in the Ethiopian teaching program who was standing outside a miserable village of mud and sticks in bright sunshine, talking about how great it was to be involved with the lives of other people. Thousands of flies were crawling over her face as she spoke, gathering in her eyes like animals at a water hole, crawling into her mouth. I can't forget that girl; she radiated a kind of inner peace and joy and dignity. How I admired the Peace Corps for its honesty in putting something so essentially horrible on the screen to advertise what one might expect in their tight exclusive club. Later, with the television off, I lay in bed and listened to the pigs banging the tin doors on their empty feeders; they sounded like a mob of striking convicts pounding their plates on the table, and it helped me to focus my mind on the fact that I was out of business.

Dear God: I Hope I Don't Have to Eat Dogs

It was still a few days before I could climb out of my grave and begin to think of the future, and it was two weeks before I picked up a Peace Corps application at the post office and set it on the table and then walked around it warily without touching it for ten days as though it were a bomb ready to explode (as indeed it might have), trying to convince myself that at my age the idea of Peace Corps duty was foolhardy.

All of this happened, I might as well admit, at a time of real crisis for me. After 16 years of farming in the Sacramento Valley, I had finally come to the verge of bankruptcy, and with hogs selling at 12 cents a pound, was not making enough to even pay for their feed, let alone mine.

Somehow for me, it was easy in the day to disguise reality, but at night I would awaken at 3 a.m., completely vulnerable to that list of unpaid bills that passed before my eyes, to find a real and cruel reality in the situation. After about 30 nights of this, I could accept even in the daylight hours the idea that I was through as a farmer and that I must find a new way to live.

But what the hell does a bankrupt farmer do, and a middle-aged one at that? I reviewed the possibilities, filled out civil service forms, took exams for postal employment, and explored with sweet and subtle letters the possibility of working for my father who had been predicting for years that I would end just as I was indeed ending.

But all these solutions left a dry taste in my mouth, and so, one terrible night of high winds and driving rain, really without willing it with the mind alone but with every tattered nerve, I sat down, took the pen from my Levi jacket, and began to fill out the Peace Corps application. I had one reservation: "Dear God, don't send me to a country where I have to eat dogs."

The Peace Corps application is about 12 pages long, and it takes hours to fill out, requiring the applicant (at least, in my case for I am somewhat weighted in years) that he reexamine and record a thousand half-forgotten memories, many of them not too pleasant. You have to disinter and expose to eyes you will never see your entire life, your failures along with whatever talents you hope to dangle before the Peace Corps people as bait.

I airmailed my document to Washington the next day, and then I waited. I waited a month, and nothing happened. I waited another month, and nothing happened. Finally one morning, in a state of anguish, out in front of an empty mailbox, I made another pact and prayed again, "Well, okay then, God, just don't let them send me to a country where I have to eat RAW dog." And I went back to the hog pens and waiting another month.

The letter from the Peace Corps, which arrives one day and announces that you are being invited for training is, I am sure, programmed to arrive after your first enthusiasm had died and after you have already committed yourself to some other project. But there it lay one morning in my mailbox, and I opened it, already convinced that it contained rejection. I had trained myself to open it with steady fingers and a yawn on my face.

The rebirth of that original enthusiasm from this one-page letter is due to a miracle of technology—for the signature of the Peace Corps Director is so cleverly reproduced that it has every appearance of having been personally affixed to the invitation.

It is the personal quality of this signature that burst you open. I was flooded with visions of Mr. Shriver (then director of the Peace Corps) sitting at a desk in Washington studying my application along with hundreds of others and finally pointing to mine, which his associates group around him nodded in violent agreement and broke into wild yips of joy.

I held this vision in my mind as long as I could; it was very comforting, this illusion that a relationship existed between Mr. Shriver and myself. "He needs me," I kept telling myself incredulously, and I couldn't help comparing the spirit of this invitation with my only other invitation to join the Government, which arrived one day many years ago. It was signed by Franklin D. Roosevelt, and began, "Greetings." This time, I discovered that I was trembling with joy.

In spite of what the Peace Corps may feel, it is from the moment of receiving the letter that your actual Peace Corps participation begins. It is a curious and strangely intense time, since all the things and people you have lived with must suddenly be reappraised and said goodbye to—the chickens in the yard, the olive trees, the cat, the school kids who come over on Saturdays, even Mrs. Yeager's guinea hens who sneak across the road to steel hog feed. An immediate withdrawal from the scenes of the present commences, and you begin to live in the future.

It took me years to realize that that day, which I had considered the worst day of my life . . . had been the luckiest. Spewed out of that deadening rural life, screaming with rage and self-pity, as bloody and battered as a new born child, I was given another chance at a brand new kind of life. ◉

Sources

Thomsen, Moritz. "Ambassador in Levis." *Red Bluff Daily News*, June 22, 1944

———. 1969. *Living Poor*. Seattle: University of Washington Press.

———. 1978. *The Farm on the River of Emeralds*. Boston: Houghton Mifflin.

———. 1991. *The Saddest Pleasure*. Great Britain: Sumach Press.

———. 1996. *My Two Wars*. South Royalton, VT: Steerforth Press.

Wood, Justin. *Cenotaph/Moritz Thomsen House [2016]*. justinrwood.com/projects/the-moritz-thomsen-house/

1925 Rand McNally map showing the Sacramento Valley Loop from Red Bluff in the north and Sacramento to the south.

The Sacramento Valley Loop Sign Controversy

Michael McCarty

The "Sacramento Valley Loop" consisted of two separate highway routes whereby travelers from the north heading south could reach Sacramento either via the westside state highway (99W) or the eastside state highway (99E). Red Bluff was the northern terminus (which met at Main and Oak Streets) and Sacramento was the southern terminus of both routes. Needless to say, there was a constant battle between towns on 99W and 99E to bring travelers down their respective route. Service stations, restaurants/cafes and hotels/motels ALL wanted to supplement their business with tourist dollars.

The "players" involved (so to speak) were Los Molinos, Chico, Durham, Gridley, Live Oak, Marysville, Wheatland, and Roseville for 99E and Proberta, Corning, Orland, Artois, Willows, Maxwell, Williams, Arbuckle, Dunnigan, and Woodland for 99W. But for Red Bluff, it was a win/win situation because regardless which route tourists took, they had to go through Red Bluff since the state highway went through the city. It would be another 40 plus years before this would change with the building of I-5, which went to the east of downtown.

East Versus West

The squabbling between the cities and counties wasn't solving anything. It was time to put away their differences and work together for the greater good:

> Two thousand machines loaded with tourists will enter California everyday next summer over the state highway from Oregon, in the opinion of Harvey Toy, chairman of the state highway commission, and Chico business men are already beginning to arise the question of how to attract a substantial number of these tourists down the east side highway and into Chico.
>
> The directors of the Chico Chamber of Commerce discussed at their last meeting the best methods to pursue to bring the tourists through Chico, and plans are underway to cooperate with Marysville and the other east side communities in advertising the east side highway. A move has been started to join with the communities of the west side in erecting large signs which will advertise both the east and west side highways as the Sacramento Valley Loop. Two signs will be erected, one above the junction of the road at Red Bluff, and the other at a point below Sacramento. W. D. Walker of the Hotel Oaks and A. G. Eames, president of the Chamber of Commerce, are working together to bring about erection of these signs as soon as possible. (*Chico Record*, January 19, 1924)

Chico, along with every other community on the east side highway, was more than eager to get a piece of the "tourist pie" from the expected 2,000 travelers from the north. Plans were in the works to involve their west side colleagues to build two billboard signs, one at or near Red Bluff and the other near the state capitol.

Representatives of each of the seven counties involved discussed ideas as to how to divide these expected tourist dollars evenly between the two routes. One idea envisioned was a placement of a billboard above Red Bluff 116 feet long!!! This would make this "super" billboard 38.6 yards long!! It would be an impressive sight to behold indeed for the traveler. The other topic discussed was an information bureau above Red Bluff.

> Yesterday's discussion was given over to the problem of ways and means of distributing the traffic over both the east and west side roads and of influencing the tourists to stop in the Sacramento

valley long enough to gain an appreciation of the productiveness and the points of interest in the Northern California section.

Two plans were suggested by W. D. Walker, chairman of the seven counties road sign committee. The first plan to be given consideration is the erection of two huge sign boards, one above Red Bluff and the other below Sacramento. The signs would picture in details the picturesque valley. The second plan is the establishment of a tourists information bureau above Red Bluff where information of the general nature can be given the travelers. Both plans received the approval of all those present.

A miniature sign depicting the Sacramento Valley Loop road was offered as an exhibition by Walker in order to explain the plan under consideration. The sign when constructed above Red Bluff and below Sacramento will be 116 feet long and 16 feet high and the painting will be of such proportions that the principal cities, valleys, hills and streams, and products of the communities will be shown in colors and easily discernible by the motorists from the road.

It is for the purpose of getting an even distribution of this huge amount of tourist traffic and giving the tourist themselves an opportunity of knowing the opportunities that await them in the Sacramento Valley. That the leaders in the communities of both east and west side band themselves together in an effort to disseminate information to the travelers.

In addition to the signs, Walker advocates the establishment of an information bureau at some point above Red Bluff where the tourist may stop and get detailed information about the kind of country he is about to travel through. The persons on duty at the bureau would be impartial in their descriptions of the east and west side and would have printed matter for distribution to the traveler. The upkeep of the bureau would be the borne by the businessmen of both the east and west sides. There is a hundred million dollar tourist crop in California.

R. H. Boding, secretary of the Chamber of Commerce at Red Bluff testifies, "Red Bluff has been in a particular situation. For we have not wanted to favor either side of the valley in directing traffic southward. As a result we have had to confine ourselves to telling the traveler the mileage of each road and the condition of each highway and let him choose for himself which road to take. (*Chico Record*, February 9, 1924)

In this next meeting, a discussion was held about installing an "illuminating" sign above Main Street in Red Bluff at the point where "east meets west."

> Thirty-four representatives of the counties involved met to discuss the questions involved at the Tremont Hotel in Red Bluff as the guests of the RB Chamber of Commerce.
>
> Representatives entered into the discussion and while there were some differences of opinions as to the best methods to be employed, the sentiment was unanimous that the presence of the various signs "already" in place seeking to divert travel to one particular place or route, should be replaced by one general sign, unbiased in its attempt to attract notice to the several communities and the valley as a whole
>
> T. H. Ramsey of Red Bluff, advanced the idea that an illuminated sign put across Main street in RB at a point where the east and west side highways diverge, would result in a lessening confusion in the minds of the tourists and that permission for such a sign probably could be had from the city authorities, providing the wording was fair to both sides of the valley. (*Chico Record*, February 16, 1924)

About a week later another meeting was held to discuss costs:

> A. G. Eames, figured the two signs would cost approximately $2,000, a restroom and the information another $2,000, with additional $1,000 expense for distribution of literature. Walker suggested a smaller loop sign and to spend the remainder of the money for a comfortable room and information bureau. (*Red Bluff Sentinel and Weekly News*, February 22, 1924)

There was a debate as to where should that monster sign be placed as well as the information bureau. One thought was about four miles north of Red Bluff. However, the Red Bluff Chamber of Commerce had a different idea.

The Red Bluff Chamber of Commerce presented a request that the "loop" sign soon to be erected on the highway be located at the edge of that city instead of several miles north and that the distribution of literature be centered at Red Bluff instead of the location first agreed upon. The sign committee will give due consideration to this request. (*Chico Record*, April 25, 1924)

An agreement about placement was finally reached after several months:

Committee from Chico Chamber of Commerce, Red Bluff Business men's Association and the city trustees here were in complete accord at the conference in Red Bluff Thursday evening over the question of placing a Sacramento Valley Loop map [sign]. Messrs. Eames, Walker and Grady of Chico declared the map (sign) should be established just where the people of this city wanted it and they would, they said, be pleased to abide by whatever decision was reached. Local business men probably will ask the map (sign) be placed at a point not far north of red Bluff.

The map [sign], however, will not be established until after the proposed valley loop sign is placed at Main and Oak streets in Red Bluff. City Engineer W. F. Luning is to prepare plans for this sign which will be erected at the earliest practicable time. With this accomplished all the signs north of Red Bluff which direct traffic over either the east or west side highways will be removed and eliminate much friction the signs have caused. (*Red Bluff Sentinel and Weekly News*, June 20, 1924)

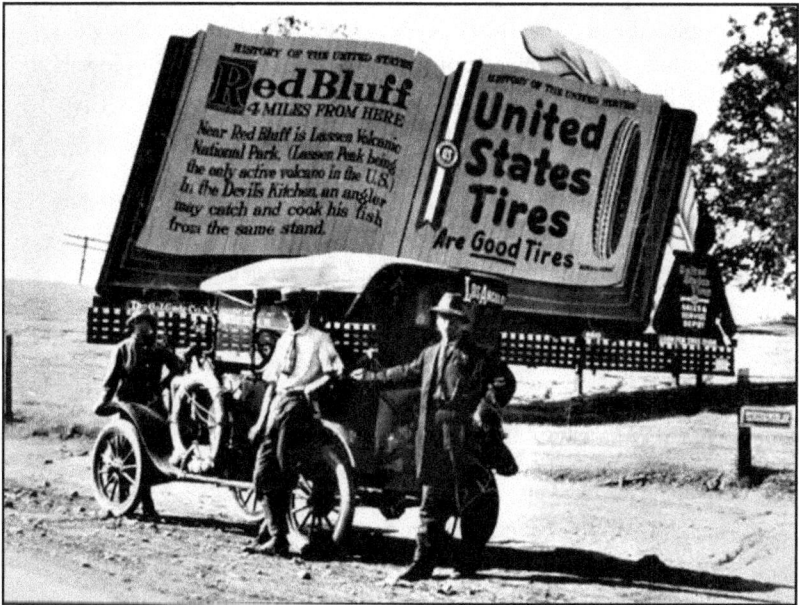

This is NOT the 116-foot sign, but it states, "Red Bluff 4 miles from here'." This American Tire Company billboard would have been seen by those traveling south to Red Bluff. The photo was taken between 1921-1927 (the 1921 laid slab top on US99 can be seen and the 2.5 ft asphalted shoulders have not been added as of yet; work on the shoulders was started in the latter part of 1927).

This meeting is significant in that the idea of a 16-foot sign and building an information bureau had been dropped. Efforts were now directed towards a sign being suspended across Main and Oak Streets in Red Bluff.

Where the East Meets the West

The electric sign that was to proudly hang above the junction of Main and Oak Streets arrived from its manufacture two and a half months later.

> The 28 x 6 foot electric sign which will be erected at Red Bluff to advertise the Sacramento Valley Loop - both the east and west side highways - has been delivered by the San Francisco firm constructing it. It was purchased by the seven county committee. (*Sacramento Bee*, September 3, 1924)

This more compact size would let motorists see the message more easily. With the new sign now in the possession of the city, it was time to install it.

> The work has been started of the erecting the Sacramento Valley Loop sign at Main and Oak streets, this city, which when completed will direct the large volume of traffic passing through Red Bluff to either the east or west side state highways. Employees of the Pacific Gas and Electric Co., are doing the work under the direction of city Engineer W. F. Luning. The cost will be approximately $1,000.
>
> The big sign is to be 21 feet above the street and suspended by cables from towers on both sides of the thoroughfare. The sign will be six feet in height and contain about eighty electric globes. The main letters of the sign are to be sixteen inches in height. (*Chico Record*, September 10, 1924)

The next order of business was to lay the concrete foundations for the two support towers that would hold up this impressive 28 x 6 feet electrified sign high above the NE and NW corners of Main and Oak Streets.

> The first section of concrete foundations for the Sacramento Valley highway "Loop" sign at Red Bluff is complete and work will resume in a few days to complete the erection of the large guide sign, according to word received by Theodore Grady, Jr., secretary of the Chamber of Commerce, from H. B. Heryford, manager of the west side division of the Pacific Gas and Electric Co. (*Chico Record*, September 20, 1924)

The Sacramento Valley Loop sign at Main and Oak Streets in Red Bluff.

The vision of A.G. Eame and seven counties in joining together was coming to fruition with the new ideas for the Sacramento Valley loop sign. Everyone hoped the sign would cause tourists to travel one highway and then travel the other one back. This way, communities on both highways would benefit.

Some fascinating facts in great details of the new sign and improved towers can be gleaned from the newspapers reporting on the progress of the installation:

> A new Sacramento Valley Loop sign for directing travelers over the east and west side highways from Red Bluff will be placed at an early date at the intersection of Main and Oak streets, where two roads diverge. Work has been started drilling holes in the concrete foundation of the present steel towers from which the big electric sign is to be suspended across the street. Four holes at each tower will be drilled at the depth of three feet in the concrete to receive three- fourths inch steel bars which are to extend up the rear side of the towers.
>
> These steel towers, with the reinforcement, will all be encased in concrete, making concrete columns, or parts, to support the sign. The columns will be 29 feet high, 36 inches square at the base and 21 inches square at the top.
>
> The sign is 20 feet long and 6 feet wide (high). When erected the bottom of the sign will be 18 feet above the crown of Main

street. There will be a galvanized steel bracket 8 feet long on each tower placed 20 feet above the street. The bottom of the sign will be guyed with cables attached to these brackets to keep the sign from swaying in the event of hard winds.

The sign reads: RED BLUFF JUNCTION SACRAMENTO VALLEY LOOP. These letters are 16 inches high. The letters Red Bluff will be illuminated on both sides of the sign. The other letters will be only illuminated on the north side, as travel towards the valley comes from that direction. The sign weighs about 700 pounds. (*Red Bluff Sentinel and Weekly News*, February 6, 1925)

Two changes to the Loop sign itself are mentioned: the new sign was slightly shorter in length and instead of being 21 feet above the street, it was lowered to 18 feet and cables were attached to the bottom corners to keep it from swaying in the wind.

More detailed information as to why the sign needed to be replaced and its manufacture is explained in this article from the *Chico Record* (February 19, 1925):

The Sacramento Valley highway Loop sign erected at Red Bluff several months ago, and later dismantled at the request of the Red Bluff city officials, now is being replaced, it was announced by Theodore Grady, secretary of the Chico Chamber of Commerce before the Chico Exchange Club.

Placing of the sign at the Red Bluff location was the culmination of a movement launched by the local Chamber of Commerce several years ago at the "Hands Across the River" meeting held here, together with numerous subsequent meetings held by the committee members named at the time.

The sign was manufactured by the Federal Electric Company, but after the six by twenty-eight-foot board was installed and lighted for a short time, the supports gave way, causing the sign to sag and it was declared unsafe by the Red Bluff officials. Their orders that it be dismantled were carried out and negotiations immediately were open by the local Chamber to have it replaced.

Extended negotiations with the electric company brought the cooperation of that concern and the work of pouring concrete to reinforce the supporting standards now in progress. The work of repairing and replacing the sign will entail an expenditure of approximately $400.

Despite the poor quality, the new and improved support towers can be seen clearly in this photo holding the smaller sign. This photo dates from 1925-1927, not 1934 as mentioned in my previous article, "Highway 99E: The Missing Piece of the Puzzle" (2019 *Memories*)..

> The sign advertises both the east and west side highways and it's cost and maintenance is to be borne by the counties served by the two highways forming the Valley Loop.

Once more the city and those counties involved with their vision of the Loop sign were filled with a sense of pride and accomplishment, but not everyone was feeling the love: "Now that we have our Valley loop sign all up and screaming, it will be in order for tourists to halt and inquire what it means. Not a few Red Bluff people are asking the same question. But it's an ornament" (Red Bluff Sentinel and Weekly News, April 10, 1925)

Another debate reared its ugly head among some of the Red Bluff business men concerning a simple wordage on the sign:

> Members of the Red Bluff Chamber of Commerce are in a quandary. The sign erected at Red Bluff announcing that the city is the junction of two highways is said to be misinterpreted by tourists, who believe that the sign means that Red Bluff is merely the junction and the city proper is somewhere else.
>
> Some lively discussion was indulged in at the last meeting of the Chamber of Commerce. Red Bluff business men want that word "junction" changed. Dick Boding suggested "intersection." The sign was placed there by the towns down the valley, a monument to the desire to compose the differences of the two

sides of the valley as to tourist travel. It has cost a great deal of money and is an attractive thing.

The upshot of the discussion was instructions to the secretary to get in touch with A. G. Eames of Chico, asking his consent to make the change. The business men are willing to dig down and pay the cost. (*Chico Record*, August 29, 1925)

D. J. (Jack) Metzger

It's now 1926. The replacement Loop sign has now been proudly erected high above the terminus of the Sacramento Valley Loop for just a little over a year and everyone seemed happy until a lawsuit was filed:

> D. J. Metzger wants the towers and electric sign on Main street, near Oak street removed. He says it interferes with his view.
>
> Metzger has filed suit against the city to have the tower, which was erected by the combined efforts of Chico, Red Bluff and other cities, removed. The sign bears the words: Red Bluff, Junction of the Sacramento Valley Loop".
>
> In his complaint filed with the superior court by his counsel, J. T. Matlock, the plaintiff sets forth that the tower, which was built to obviate further contention over routing of the tourists down the east and west side highways, obstructs the view from his business property Metzger owns on NW side of Main and Oak streets.
>
> Metzger seeks to have the court adjudge that "the tower is and will be an unlawful invasion upon the property rights of this plaintiff and an interference with the free use of his property; that the defendant (the city) has not the right to maintain the tower: that an injunction be granted to the plaintiff and issued against the defendant, commanding it to remove the posts created, and that the nuisance be abated, and restore the sidewalk as it was previous to erection of the posts and further enjoining and prohibiting the defendant from hereafter erecting any structure of a similar nature in front of the property of the plaintiff upon the streets. (*Chico Record*, March 31, 1926)

Metzger's (businessman, future mayor and state senator) complaint alleges that on April 7, 1924, the city, without any right, permitted holes to be dug in the sidewalk on Main Street immediately in front of his building. His property that was on the northwest corner of Main and Oak Streets, and he claimed that the concrete pillars were a nuisance and hindered the appearance of this property."[1]

> If the city of Red Bluff is required to remove the concrete pillars on Main street, to which Jack Metzger has registered an objection, it is going to be some job. The pillars were originally steel towers, but the towers not being strong enough to support the big sign swung between them; the concrete pillars were constructed around the steel towers. The concrete foundation is considerable distance below the concrete pavement and sidewalk; were built to stay. They are the strongest kind of reinforced concrete. The pillars are about three feet square at the bottom, tapering to about a foot at the top. They are about 25 feet high. Dynamite is about the only thing that will remove them.
>
> The tower and the big sign across the street were erected at the approximate cost of $2,000. All but about $200 of this was provided by the cities in the valley below Red Bluff. Chico stood the brunt of the expense and took the initiative in establishing the sign. Red Bluff was not required to pay a cent, but did contribute $200, since some of the valley towns fell down on the agreement. (*Chico Record*, March 31, 1926)

Metzger further stated in his lawsuit that

> in the use of the building for store purposes and especially for the business now conducted there, it is necessary the sidewalk and the street in the front be maintained in a condition attractive in appearance; that the post or tower detract from the appearance of the building, shuts off the light and if allowed to remain will greatly diminish the value of the property. (*Red Bluff Sentinel and Weekly News*, April 2, 1926)

Less than a month since the lawsuit had been filed, Red Bluff suffered a set back in its attempt to get the lawsuit thrown out:

> In superior court here, Judge John F. Ellison has overruled the demurrer of the defense in the suit of D. J. Metzger against the city of Red Bluff, in which the plaintiff seeks to have removed from

---

1 Between the years of 1924 to 1926, this corner had been occupied by "Jack's Place" whose proprietor being a one G. N. Jack. Sometime in 1926, it was taken over by "Nickerson's Restaurant.

the corner of Main and Oak streets the Sacramento valley Loop sign which was erected there a couple of years ago largely through the efforts of Chico citizens. Metzger claims the sign obstructs the view from the store building which he owns at the southwest corner of Main and Oak streets and that it is a nuisance.

The defense demurred on the ground, as set forth by counsel for municipality, that the complaint of the plaintiff did not state a cause of action, Judge Ellison held in contrary and gave the defense 15 days in which to answer. (*Red Bluff Sentinel and Weekly News*, April 30, 1926)

No evidence of an answer could be found. The trial was set to start on June 23, 1926.

The mandamus[2] suit of D. J. Metzger, a local livestock buyer, against the city of Red Bluff, looking to a removal of the Sacramento Valley Loop sign at Main and Oak streets, has been set for trial in superior court here June 23. Metzger particularity objects to the word, "junction" on the sign and also declares the pillars supporting the sign obstructs the view from his property on the west side of main street. (*Red Bluff Sentinel and Weekly News*, June 11, 1926)

Between the setting of the trial to June 23, 1926, ten months had come and gone. As it is with most court cases, it was to be a long and drawn out affair:

The Wednesday afternoon session of the trial of Metzger vs. City of Red Bluff injunction suit, involving the so-called "Loop sign" opened with R. M. Norvell on the stand. In effect Norvell testified that the sign was of benefit to the traveling public. T. H. Ramsay and W. H. Fisher testified to the same effect.

R. H. Boding was called to testify as to the information the sign conveyed to the traveling public. John O'Connor testified as to putting in the base of the sign and as to payment received. E. F. Lennon, city clerk testified as to certain ordinances involving the rights of property owners as to streets and sidewalks and same were entered as evidence.

R. H. Reschar testified to hearing a conversation between G. G. Stice chairman of the board of trustees and D. J. Metzger relative

2 A lawsuit used to compel someone, such as an officer or employee of the United States government, to act on an administrative matter that is not discretionary; where they have a legal duty to do so and have not.

to the sign. According to his testimony Metzger had objected particular to the wording of the sign, but the witness could not recall that he had objected to the post. G. G. Stice was later called upon the stand and his testimony as to this conversation was about the same as that of Mr. Reschar.

Stanley Gordon, local manager for the California State Automobile Association, testified as to certain signs which had been placed on a lamp post near the present sign post, but which had been removed when new signs were placed on the concrete post supporting the sign.

The case is dragging, with numerous objections by counsel for both sides and the case is running into the third day. It is hoped that the case will be finished by Thursday. Judge Purkett of Willows is sitting in the case.

The "Loop sign" case of Metzger vs. City of Red Bluff was completed as far as evidence was concerned this morning. The argument will be submitted by briefs later.

Frank Sheridian, Harry Huber, G. N. Jack and Stanley Gordon were recalled by plaintiff for further examination. Defense attorney did not cross examine these witnesses. Owing to another case coming up arguments could not be heard at this time.

Evidence submitted this morning was in connection with the question as to the value to the traveling public of the sign in question. Gordon testified as to the value of the smaller signs. He stated that the large "Loop sign" had no connection with the organization which he represents, the California State Automobile Association. (*Red Bluff Sentinel and Weekly News*, April 1, 1927)

The Judge made his decision three months later:

Judge Claude F. Purkett of Glenn county, has handed down a decision sustaining the action of D. J. Metzger against the city of Red Bluff. Judge Purkitt cites the case of Williams vs. The Los Angeles Railway Co., and Strong vs. Sullivan bearing upon the right of a city under ordinance to maintain posts and other obstructions in front of private property. The court does deny, however, the plaintiffs claim that property owner is owner in fee to the center of the street. The property is currently occupied by L. M. Nickerson, who operates a restaurant and soft drink stand.

Whether the case will be appealed or not depends upon A. G. Eames of Chico, who was instrumental in having the sign erected. Local city officials stated today they will leave it entirely up to Mr. Eames as to future actions. (*Red Bluff Sentinel and Weekly News*, July 21, 1927)

While future action was being deliberated, Metzger made a surprise announcement:

You can tell the people of Red Bluff that I will build such a sign any place that is suitable and where I can get a permit to build it", declared Metzger. He suggested the river bridge on Oak street. When the city bonded itself to build a bridge on lower Main street, there was also a proposal on the ballot for an arch over the bridge to carry a sign of some kind. This was defeated because the added expense. (*Red Bluff Sentinel and Weekly News*, July 29, 1927)

Two locations were mentioned as new homes for the sign:

1. The Centennial Free bridge over the Sacramento River.

2. The bridge on lower Main Street (the new 210 foot Reeds Creek bridge completed in 1927). It was a RC (reinforced concrete) girder type bridge built by the Holdener Construction Company that replaced the old 275-foot steel pony truss bridge that had spanned Reeds Creek since the late 1890s. There was talk of putting an arch gateway at the north end, which was the city limits.

One month later a new trial was sought by Red Bluff under these grounds:

The city will ask the court to set aside the decision and grant a new trial on the grounds that there was insufficient evidence to justify the decision; that there was an error in the law occurring at the trial and expected to by the city, that the decision of the court was against the law. (*Red Bluff Sentinel and Weekly News*, August 5, 1927)

However, there would be no new trial, nor an appeal. It was time to throw in the towel and move on:

The famous "loop sign" at Main and Oak streets will probably come down. This was indicated when A. G. Eames stated to a news representative today that they would not appeal the case. Motion for a new trial was recently denied. The city board will probably act on the matter tonight. (*Red Bluff Sentinel and Weekly News*, September 6, 1927)

Work to remove the sign began the first week of October and it was lowered on October 17:

> Work of taking down the huge electric sign at the intersection of Main and Oak streets, advertising Red Bluff as the junction of the Sacramento Valley Loop, will commence during the first part of next week, according to B. H. Steffen, Chico contractor, who will have charge of the work. The sign itself will be taken to Chico where it has been sold and the concrete towers from which it is suspended will be levelled, according to Mr. Steffen, who is in Red Bluff today. (*Red Bluff Sentinel and Weekly News*, October 7, 1927)

> The huge electric sign at the intersection of Main and Oak street is ready to come down. The blocks and tackle are all in place and the last day of the sign is drawing near. Only the arrival of a truck from Chico, which was due here at 8:30 o'clock this morning, but which has not as yet put in an appearance, has delayed lowering the sign. Workmen began removal of the sign yesterday morning and the scaffolding was placed around the piers which support the sign in preparation for the razing of the towers. Powerful blocks and tackles were attached to the cables holding the sign in place at either end. When the truck arrives the supporting turnbuckles will be loosed and the sign dropped in the truck. (*Red Bluff Sentinel and Weekly News*, October 18, 1927)

After its removal, the sign headed to its new home and owner in Chico:

> The large electric sign which denoted Red Bluff as the junction of the Sacramento Valley Loop of highways is on its way to Chico tonight where it will become property of a Chico doctor. The sign was lowered on a truck this afternoon and hauled away and work upon the demolition of the concrete pillars which supported it will be commenced immediately. (*Red Bluff Sentinel and Weekly News*, October 19, 1927)

With the electric sign gone, the two concrete towers were also removed:

Only a few bars of steel standing upright at the corner of Oak and Main streets are all that remain of the solid concrete and steel towers which supported the huge electric sign a few weeks ago. Workmen immediately commenced work on taking down the towers which supported it. The concrete was broken into pieces and hauled away for use in other structures. The steel will be cut away with an acetylene torch soon. (*Red Bluff Sentinel and Weekly News*, November 1, 1927)

Metzger never did build a new sign, and the fate of the existing loop signs is unknown. ◉

⁓∞⁓

Michael S. McCarty was born, raised, and lives in Red Bluff. He graduated Red Bluff High in 1981 and is interested in Tehama County and WWII history. While he loves rugby, his life-long passion is the original state Highway 99 and old bridges.

There are not too many photos of the Loop sign, but it must of been quite eye catching during its heyday. This view of the sign is from the southeast corner of Main and Oak at the Associated service station. Since the bottom cables are attached, this would be sign #2

The last crossing of Jelly's Ferry just before the ribbon cutting for the new Pratt truss steel bridge on January 15, 1950. The ferry operated at this crossing for 93 years, from 1857 to 1950. In 2020, work to replace the 72-year-old bridge began at a cost of $53 million. The new bridge was dedicated November 10, 2022.

The Jelly Area of Tehama County

Tehama County Genealogical & Historical Society

The Jelly's Ferry district is located about 10 miles north of Red Bluff, along the edge of the Sacramento River. The land lies along the river where the river makes a big bend. The fertile soil, plentiful game, and its particular location were all factors in making the land a historic spot.

After the Mexican War, California became a military territory of the United States—until September 1850, when it was adopted as a state. With the coming of statehood, California received title to all lands within her boundaries that were not already privately owned.

In 1852, a man by the name of Andrew Jelly had filed squatters rights to part of the old Mexican Breisgau land grant along the Sacramento River. While Jelly was living on this land and had filed squatters rights to it, the title still remained in the hands of the state. Finally, in order to raise much needed money, the state of California divided the land into 160-acre sections and advertised the land for sale. Andrew Jelly bought several of the 160-acre sections from the state with script he had obtained from Mexican War veterans, and by direct purchase.

Andrew Jelly had left Stubensville, Ohio in 1848 and landed in San Francisco after sailing around the Horn. He had originally come to California to seek gold, but bad luck and poor timing ended his mining career. He decided to find some good land and start a farm. He chose prime farmland along the Sacramento River, just south of Battle Creek. After Jelly acquired title to the land, he immediately set up the foundations to build a permanent house on it.

Andrew Jelly realized that if the area were ever going to grow, he would have to do something to help promote travel in the area. His answer was to build a good road through the area and make a ferry to cross the river. In 1856, he built a two-story brick house that was big enough and strong enough to hold his family and travelers—65 feet long and 31 feet wide with a fireplace at each end, all on a brick foundation extending 5 feet into the ground. It would become a well-known stopping place for the stagecoaches and freight wagons, a hotel for the weary traveler, and headquarters for the Jelly Ranch.

A Chinese cook prepared meals for the travelers as well as for the family. Jelly employed a lot of Chinese in his farming. A rock wall about a mile long built by the Chinese workers can still be seen just west of Jellys Ferry Road.

Andrew Jelly's brick home (Elbert Haakonson collection).

In 1857 Andrew Jelly built a ferry for crossing the Sacramento River about a mile south of his brick house and ranch headquarters; it operated as a toll ferry until 1890 when Tehama County took it over. The county operated the ferry until it was replaced with a steel trestle bridge in 1950. The ferry and connecting road greatly benefited travel in northern Tehama County and in Shasta County, both local and passing. It served not only the north-south transportation needs, but also the settlers of the eastside foothill communities of Manton and Shingletown. At least three roads connected the two communities to the route over Jelly's Ferry and the world beyond. After the ferry was established, the California Stage Company ran a line that crossed it on the way from Sacramento to Shasta. Old billboards on display in Old Sacramento show Jelly as one of its north valley stops.

The early ferryboats were constructed of wood, and required occasional replacement, but the last ferry used was made of steel. The ferry, which was the last one in Tehama County, was an oddity. Like all Jelly ferries before it, the vessel had no engine, rather it was propelled by the current of the river. Ferry operators cranked a tethering cable around a capstan, slanting the hull slightly into the current. The water sliding along the upstream side would shove it across the 400-foot wide stream along a main trolley cable.

Another view of the Jelly home.

Jelly's ferry on the Sacramento River (TCGHS archives)

Fred Linstrum was a ferry operator for many of the early years. A newspaper article in January 1949 stated:

> the entire fleet of the Tehama County navy is scheduled to be abandoned this year and placed in moth balls—forever. The fleet is comprised entirely of the single ferry here, which is manned by a crew of three: brothers Eric and John Hunaeus and Chris Tanem. The home waters are the flow of the Sacramento River where it loops past the south of this tranquil settlement of stock ranches and fruit orchards. The free ferry forms the only link in the north-south county road where it is disconnected at one sharp convolution in the river.

With the improved access to the area, more and more people saw and became interested in the land that Mr. Jelly owned. Consequently, when Andrew decided to sell some of the land he had acquired, he received some good offers. He did sell some of the tableland he had in the area, but the area in the river bottomland was not sold for quite some time.

It has been told that Andrew Jelly would invite friends from out of town to come for a game of poker. He reportedly was known to bet exorbitant amounts in some of these games. It was at one of these games, that supposedly a gentleman named Charles E. Fish got the betting rather high,

Jelly's ferry carrying sheep (TCGHS archives).

causing all the other men except for Mr. Jelly to fold their hands. Mr. Jelly called Mr. Fish's hand by betting the land on the east side of the river just where it makes a big bend. Mr. Jelly thought the land was equal in value to what Mr. Fish had bet. Mr. Fish won the hand and collected title to the land. How much truth there is to this story is unknown. If it is true, the winnings and losses were "all in the family," as research shows that Charles Fish was married to a stepdaughter of Andrew Jelly. Other information indicates that in 1886, Andrew Jelly deeded his property to his son Frank and his son-in-law Charles E. Fish, and they divided it among themselves.

County surveyor, W. F. Luning, marked out the division in 1893. Charles Fish and his wife, Margaret, took over the portion with the brick house while Frank and his wife remained in the house they had built to the east of the Jellys Ferry Road, where they would continue their hay and livestock operation with help of their sons.

Charles Fish did not build any buildings or make any real improvements on the property. He did run cattle on the land for about six of the nine years he owned it. He did break the soil on the property in one place—the north section of land that formed the bend in the river, where he planted a crop of spearmint. He even had a few llama imported into the area to eat the weeds between the tender mint leaves. But, as the llama ate away at the weeds, the grasshoppers ate away at the mint leaves. Mr. Fish lost his investment and decided to give up trying to grow any crop on the land. He decided to put the 550 acres of land up for sale, since it had been a continual drain to his funds. On February 6, 1895, Charles E. Fish made a "contract for sale" with Rev. H. L. Haakonson.

Rev. Haakonson was born in Norway and immigrated to Wisconsin. While in Wisconsin he decided he wanted to come west and start a Lutheran colony. His family and a few other families from the Lutheran Church made the two and one-half month trip across the United States in 1894. The families traveled by mule or oxen-drawn covered wagons.

Reverend Haahon Lauritz Haakonson (TCGHS archives).

As soon as the families got to California, they began to look for a location for the colony. They wanted some land in the north part of the state because it had the more temperate climate. While in the city of Chico, Rev. Haakonson heard of some land for sale along the Sacramento River some 120 miles north of Sacramento. He went to see the land and then immediately set up an agreement with the owner.

After the acquisition of some 700 acres of land, the difficult task of setting up the colony began. The Reverend's idea of a religious colony withered as all the people who were supposed to come failed to do so. Unable to manage the 700 acres by himself, he had it subdivided into mostly small 20-acre parcels and launched the Saron Fruit Colony. It is said he picked the name "Saron" as a variant of Sharon, a name appearing in the Bible and meaning a plain or valley.

Rev. Haakonson had no problem selling—all the parcels were sold within the first two years they were offered. Small farmers bought most of the parcels because the biggest contained only 75 acres. Rev. Haakonson kept the 50 acres with his house and orchard because "it was where he belonged." Early buyers of these parcels included: N. T. Heaton, Jim Emerson, Carl Lundblad, Generious Tanem, Gilbrand Hanson, Martin Simson, John Anderson, and Knute Torrison. While Haakonson did not live to see his dreams of a fruit-growing area materialize, his wife and children and neighbors planted trees and tended them; the Saron Fruit Colony did become a reality and has been primarily a fruit growing area ever since.

A unique feature of Haakonson's subdivision was how he handled the "non-plowable" land that he purchased from Fish. There is about 330 acres of it—about 160 acres of flood-prone land bordering the river for 2 miles, the remainder a rocky oak-covered hill best suited for grazing. He set up the Saron Pasture Land Corporation in which purchasers of Saron Colony land held shares proportional to the amount they purchased. The corporation gave the shareholders grazing rights to the corporation property. The shares could be passed on to new owners only with the sale of their farmland. The arrangement proved to be an effective means of preserving the land from any type of development.

The Saron Fruit Colony soil built up through the centuries by periodic flooding of the Sacramento River. That is what gave it rich 30-foot-deep Columbia Silt Loam soil. Twice in the 20th century most of the colony was inundated. In December 1937 a severe flood struck the north valley area, and the Saron Fruit Colony was under water. Then three years later, in February of 1940, it was under water again. Since construction of Shasta Dam [in Shasta County], extensive flooding has not occurred.

But the colony is still cut off from the outside occasionally in wet years. A deep slough crosses the road leading in from the east, and the wet-year high water inevitably cuts off access over it. Because of high flood control releases from Shasta Dam, the road cut-off situation may last for days and weeks. The Tehama County Road Department has attempted to correct the situation by diking the slough. However, that has met with failure. Every time a peak flood flow has occurred the dike has washed out.

Rev. Haakonson contributed funds to help build the area's first school in 1896 on an acre of land he had set aside for that purpose. The deed was recorded in December 1898. The first teacher was a Miss Albright. The class of 1903 had 17 students, and Miss Lena F. Dale was the teacher. Miss Arta

Ford taught at this school in the 1910s. She had previously taught at the Blossom School on Beegum Road. She later became the wife of Theodore Haakonson, son of Rev. Haakonson. In 1944 the school was closed, and the children were bussed to the Bend school some 10 miles away. The Reverend held church in the school on Sundays; and it didn't matter whether you were a Lutheran or not, he welcomed all.

He often brought the mail in from town and distributed it among the residents. The porch of a neighbors' house was the post office for several years. A post office was officially established in 1901 with Frank L. Jelly serving as the first postmaster. He would distribute the mail from his home. Emma M. Bacon [Mrs. A. J. McDevitt] became the postmaster in January 1916. The post office was discontinued in 1934.

In 1906, Jose Lourenco, a Portuguese immigrant began to purchase property in the Saron Colony. He first bought the Hanson property, then the Tanem, Anderson and Simonson properties, on which he raised fruit, hay and livestock. This property passed to his two sons, Frank Lourence and William "Bill" Lawrence after Jose's death in 1956. Bill still farms his property with his son, Marvin; and Frank, who died in 1971, passed his 60-acre parcel, which was planted in alfalfa, prunes, walnuts, apricots, and peaches to his four children, Eugenia, Fred, Patricia, and Richard.

Jose Lourenco operated the Jelly's Ferry store at the west end of the Saron Colony Road, selling general merchandise, groceries, and gasoline during the late 1910s and into the 1920s. Someone only needed to ring the bell in the store it they wanted service. The building no longer remains.

From the time when the Rev. Haakonson divided the land not much has changed except for the riverbank. The peach trees still produce some peaches, but prunes had replaced many of those peaches by 1920. During the 1920s the population in the area was around 15 families; but in fruit harvest season it would double. The main crops then were sun-dried peaches and prunes. The men would usually do the peach picking, and women and children would cut the fruit and place the pitted halves on wooden trays. When filled with fruit, the trays were loaded onto flanged-wheel rail cars and pushed into sulphur houses where burning sulphur would fumigate the fruit overnight. From there, the trays would be spread in the dry yard for about a week. The dried peaches would be scraped off, put in sacks and hauled to market.

Prunes were harvested by hand-knocking them off the trees. Then they were picked off the ground and transported to a dipper, where they were dipped for a few seconds in scalding lye water. They were then placed on trays and spread out in the sun to dry for about a week. This was generally a job for men, women, and children.

Rev. H. L. Haakonson left his house and property to his son, Theodore. Theodore continued to run the farm and grow crops and was a successful farmer. He remodeled the old brick Jelly house and built a large barn and garage near the house. He continued to make improvements on the home and land until he left it to his son, Elbert who still owns the property.

The Jelly Ranch in later years contained 2,000 acres. Frank Sr. had built a white frame ranch house about a mile north of the ferry in 1889 for his bride-to-be Elizabeth Long, daughter of Joseph Long. Frank and Elizabeth still lived there in 1949. Frank Jelly had sons, Andrew Joseph and Frank Elmer, who married in 1945 to Marian Nunes, the daughter of Antone Nunes. When interviewed in 1949, Frank Sr. still performed a full day's work every day in the caring of his livestock and the 300-bottomland acres of grain grown for their feed.

The county road passing in front of the Jelly Ranch is reportedly part of an old Oregon Trail over which traveled stock and stages during the gold rush era. There was still evidence of an old wagon trail, though long abandoned, which ran from the ferry crossing east across the Jelly Ranch in the direction of Inks Creek. Parts of the old trail showed hard use; in some places large volcanic rocks embedded in the earth showed considerable wear. This wear was undoubtedly from lumber wagons, which were used to carry the better lumber from "The Dump" at the end of the Blue Ridge Flume to Jelly's Ferry. Frank stated the trail was already out of use before his father Andrew arrived. The Jelly ranching operation ended in the early 1960s when Frank, Elizabeth, Joe, and Elmer all died within a seven-year period. Marian sold the ranch to Richard B. Richmond in the mid-1960s.

Richmond was a San Francisco cannery owner who ran an intensive cattle operation until a few years later when he died. After his death the ranch was surveyed and divided into two parcels and sold. Charles Orwick bought one and Vincent Flynn the other. Orwick combined several ranches that extend from the Jelly's Ferry bridge north to Battle Creek. He launched into a large cattle operation and planted row crops on the Jelly portion. In the 1990s

Charles sold most of the original Jelly family estate to the Bureau of Land Management. The Flynns developed their tract into an extensive walnut orchard, which they later sold to Sam and Barbara Mudd.

Like the general trend of farming elsewhere, the land tracts in the Saron Fruit Colony have tended to consolidate into larger units, though the trend has not been as extensive as it might have been. Some of the Saron Pasture Land Corporation has been sold to the Bureau of Land Management. ◎

Source

Tehama County Genealogical & Historical Society's *150 Years of Tehama County History,* available at TehamaCountyHistory.com.

Frank Jelly standing at gate, c. 1900 (Tehama County Library archives)

Photo taken at Saddle Camp in 1942 before a road was built to Tomhead Lookout. Ed Henderson's pack string is loaded with steel beams to be used to build a new forest service lookout on Tomhead Mountain. All material for the lookout had to be packed in by mules (Anita Henderson Gonzalez collection)

Tomhead Mountain and Saddle Camp

Tehama County Genealogical & Historical Society

Tomhead Mountain lies in the Coast Range Mountains on the north side of the South Fork of Cottonwood Creek Canyon. This area is located west of Red Bluff in the Shasta-Trinity National Forest. Tomhead Mountain (elevation 6,754 feet) has for many years been the site of a forest service lookout. In fact, it is one of the few manned forest service lookouts in operation in western Tehama County today. Just under the mountain peak are the Tomhead Saddle Campground and the trailhead to the Yolla Bolly Wilderness Area.

According to an early Forest Service District Ranger, C. K. St. John, the story was told by James B. Dyer, who lived on the Old Stevenson Place, of how the mountain received its name. Dyer's story was

> that in very early days, there was an old man, who in prior times lived on his [Dyer's] home site. This old man, who prospected and hunted for his living, was named Tom. No one knew much about the fellow as he kept very much to himself; in fact, no one even knew his last name. His chin was very long and sharp, and his mouth sunken, presenting a very striking appearance. From Dyer's

place, Tomhead Mountain resembled the features of old Tom to such an extent that gradually it became known as Tom's Head. In later years it was shortened by the residents and became the official name that appears as such on all maps.

On the north side of Tomhead Mountain is an area known as Saddle Camp. It is located about 42 miles west of Red Bluff and can be reached by taking the Pettyjohn Road. The Humboldt Trail passed through this area and so did the valley sheepmen and cattlemen, when they drove their livestock to the Yolla Bolly area in the Coast Range Mountains for summer feed.

An excerpt from an article in the *Red Bluff Daily News* dated, Friday, August 10, 1960, written by Sam Ehorn stated:

> About the year 1900, [Lou] Bayles and George Kraft took one of the first bands of sheep up to Tomhead Mountain, driving them all the way. At that time the county road was completed only to Cold Fork Creek, better known as the Pettyjohn Place. From there on was a dim trail and lots of brush. They drove them up to Greasewood Hill and there turned them over to Luke Raglin, who took them on up the mountain and over to Yolla Bolly.
>
> The cattlemen also took a good many cattle to the mountains in those days. Bayles also helped with cattle drives and that same year he helped Troughton take some cattle up the mountain."

The first area to be called Saddle Camp was at Alva Tracy's cabin, later owned by Alonzo and Annie Swain. It was in 1907, when this area was opened up, by the extension of the Pettyjohn Road to Alva Tracy's cabin, and the "Saddle Camp" area began to see much activity. This place became the old trailhead to the Yolla Bolly country. Some people say that Saddle Camp received its name because, to get beyond that point in the Coast Range Mountains, you had to "camp" and "saddle-up," as that was the end of the wagon road.

In June 1906, the California and Massachusetts Copper Mines Company purchased a number of private mining claims on Tomhead Mountain near Saddle Camp. The mines were easily reached from the "rancho" of Alva Tracy, who had lived in the district for some years and was a miner and prospector of experience. These private claims were owned by S. C. Shadwell, Eugene Burrill, Alva Tracy, and J. O. Halley. The newly formed mining district was known as the Red Bluff Mining District. It was thought that this copper mine in Tehama County would prove to be of great benefit to Red Bluff merchants and the community in general. In fact, in October 1907, the California and Massachusetts Copper Mines Company was looking to secure the co-operation of the state highway department to connect Eureka with the Sacramento Valley by way of the Tomhead mines. Because of the railroad system's expensive transportation rates, the company had planned to secure a wagon road to tidewater at Humboldt Bay. Over this wagon road they would have hauled coke [fuel made from coal] and supplies from Eureka, and from the mines, they would take the ore to a possible smelter to be located at the bay. These plans did not materialize, and the road from the Tomhead Mine to Eureka was never built, probably due to the frequently fluctuating price of ore and the low copper content. But the copper mine was in production for several years, and a cookhouse, cabins, and outbuildings were built for the workers to use. The Tomhead Mine was abandoned in 1918. On *Metsker's Tehama County* map a Tomhead Mine is still shown near Saddle Camp.

During the same time period as the mining on Tomhead Mountain, Frank Wilson and his family lived on his homestead on Cold Fork Creek. Frank's sons, Arthur and Judson, started a sawmill in the Saddle Camp area, which some people say was known by the locals as "The Mill." The sawmill cut a considerable amount of fine timber, and the lumber, delivered to the valley, sold for $10 a thousand board feet. It is assumed that the nearby copper mine bought lumber for their development from the Wilson Mill. The mill and a large cookhouse were located on the south side of the road at Saddle Camp, and a bunkhouse was on the north side.

Apparently with the mine and mill both operating and with several families living in the Saddle Camp area, they found a need for a school. A petition for a new school district at Saddle Camp was granted by the Board of Supervisors in February 1907 and Saddle Camp School District shows up for the first time on the Department of Education's records for the school year of 1907-08. The teacher was Miss Anna B. Healey, and the clerk trustee was Alva Tracy. There are no records stating where the school was located or which months it was in session, but because Saddle Camp School was located in the mountains, it probably was a summer school. A summer school held its vacation in December, January and February because of the deep snow and poor roads. At different times, Alva Tracy, William E. Swain, Tom Burrill, Charles Burrill, Alonzo Swain, Arthur N. Blake, Arthur

D. Wilson, George A. Hayes, James S. Linton, Louis M. Bayles, and Mrs. Thomas "Laura" Brownlee were all trustees for the school district.

The Saddle Camp School was listed on the Department of Education's records through the school year 1918-19. No further records were found past that date. It appears that 1918-19 was the time period when the employment at the sawmill and copper mine was coming to an end, so the few families that lived at Saddle Camp probably moved away.

Later a Trinity National Forest Guard Station was located near the mill site, but on the north side of the road. The Saddle Camp name then became associated with this Guard Station. Some people believe the original Saddle Camp Guard Station was located at Alva Tracy's cabin, which was about 1 mile west of the mill. Tracy was probably the first forest service ranger in the Saddle Camp area, as he held the position of District Ranger in the Trinity National Forest from 1918 through 1934. Over the years, many different men manned the Saddle Camp Guard Station. Lester Gaddis was the forest ranger at Saddle Camp in 1930, and in 1939 Lester Burrill and Clay Hendricks were working there.

Today the best remembered "Saddle Camp" was the Guard Station near the mill site. There are no remains of the mill, its buildings, or the Guard Station at Saddle Camp. But on the south side of the road is a government weather device, the only recognizable landmark, where the busy little settlement of Saddle Camp was once located. There are also several private summer cabins in the area surrounding Saddle Camp. ◉

Source

Tehama County Genealogical & Historical Society's *150 Years of Tehama County History*, available at TehamaCountyHistory.com.

African Methodist Episcopal Church (A.M.E.)

Built at a cost of $504 and dedicated on January 28, 1877. It was located on Crittenden Street in Red Bluff.

Black Pioneers in Tehama County

G. Alice Jackson

The Central Pacific Railroad was completed to Red Bluff in 1871. A depot was built on the east side of the tracks at Madison and Walnut streets. The first round house was built at the intersections of Monroe and Oak Streets and could hold two locomotives. It was later replaced by a larger one a block long, between Hickory and Cedar Streets. In 1916 the railroad's division station was moved to Gerber according to Tehama County 1856-2006 150 Years of Photos and History, published by the Tehama County Genealogical and Historical Society.

It was about this time that the number of Blacks in the county began to shrink as many of them moved to Alameda, Yolo and San Francisco Counties. Previous to this, the Everett Hunt Railroad employed many Blacks as porters, dining car cooks, and waiters. By the 1930s, the Black population of the Red Bluff area had dwindled to about fifty, the majority of whom were related to the Black pioneers. By the time my family moved to Tehama County in 1964, there were very few left. Some of the better known ones still here were Everett "Shine" Hunt and Dick Hyde. Both of these men were well liked and worked in the slaughtering industry. Dave Minch, their boss, furnished Dick Hyde, his wife, Lilly, and their son, Maurice, a place to live on the Minch ranch after Dick retired. While Dick worked for Minch, his family lived within walking distance of the plant in a rented house.

Everett Hunt came to Tehama County when many Blacks were leaving. He arrived in California with a Wild West show and bulldogged with the first RCA rodeos, according to his obituary (August 9, 1974). He worked on many ranches in the area and was very well liked. He also was employed for ten years by the Fish and Wildlife Service. He was born January 3, 1905, in North Carolina and died August 6, 1974, in Red Bluff. He was buried in Oak Hills Cemetery (OHC) in Red Bluff.

The majority of early Blacks to Tehama County were farmers who settled on free land in the outlying areas or worked on the farms of others. In general, these were the ones who moved toward the Bay area before the Blacks who settled in Red Bluff. The ones in town were primarily skilled domestics such as barbers, cooks, laundresses, and mid-wives. Some opened businesses and quite a few stayed and lived out their lives in Tehama County. Many were interred in Oak Hills Cemetery in Red Bluff and the families of some who left the county brought their loved ones back for burial here also.

In general the "Black Pioneers" to Tehama County moved here with many skills, as noted in their occupations listed in census and voter registrations: barber, blacksmith, bootblack, brick mason, butcher, cannery worker, carpenter, cook, drayman, dress maker, express man, farmer, harness maker, farrier, horse trainer, janitor, janitorial service owner, laborer, laundress, mail man, minister, mill hand, porter, restaurateur-hotel operator, shoe maker, shoe repairman (shoe refiner), stock raiser, trapper, waiter, and women's nurse (mid-wife).

The 1936 telephone book listed nine of the remaining Black individuals with phones living in the general area of Madison, Monroe, Jackson, Union, and Breckenridge streets: Mrs. J. S. Brooks, Joseph Clinton, C. O. Coffey, Miss. Sarah Fenwick, Frank Holman, Mrs. Mae Holman, two G. H. Martins, and B.F. Mitchell. The 1949 directory listed Olive Brooks, Sarah Francis Fenwick, Frank W. Holman and wife Jennie May, and Charles Mitchell.

Interesting Newspaper Articles from the Past

As shown in the following excerpts, the local papers kept the citizens of Tehama aware of what was going on around them, both good and bad. They even kept track of what others thought and wrote about.

Weekly Sentinel, November 18, 1871:

> Can It Be So — We hear it rumored on the streets that there is an
> organized Vigilance Committee, and also a band of the KKKs., in
> our quiet little town. Bah! We say to all such talk. In the first place
> we have laws, if properly administered to protect our citizens from
> the ravages of roughs. And as for the KKKs., we would advise
> he, she, or they, whoever they may be that attempted to frighten
> someone by such silly ebulations [sic] as has been indulged
> for a few days past, to bathe their head with a weak solution of
> chamomile tea, take something warm, and retire from the contest.

Weekly Sentinel, March 3, 1877:

> A Dark Transaction — A case was on trial before Justice Comstock
> during the week wherein a Colored individual was tried for
> shooting a white man. It came out in the evidence that the white
> man had hung up his coat and shot a hole in it then had darkie
> arrested for shooting him. The latter proved that he was miles away
> from the place at the time the shooting was alleged to have taken
> place. The whole matter grew out of a land dispute.

Weekly People's Cause, September 20, 1879:

> The Negro exodus from the South does not decrease in the least.
> On the contrary, there are now not less than 20,000 applications
> for laborers coming mostly from the western and north western
> States. This hegira may not affect the solid South directly, but if the
> Negros continue to leave there in large numbers, the membership
> in congress, after the next census, will be very materially lessened.
> The wiser and more conservative elements of the South have
> warned their less considerate friends, that unless the persecutions
> of the Negro is [sic] abandoned the Democracy of the South would
> in a few years loose its power, not only in the South but also in
> Congress.

Weekly People's Cause, June 12, 1880:

> *(The following was re-printed from the* San Francisco Elevator, *a Negro
> newspaper. The* Elevator *is available on microfilm from the Library of Congress. It
> was considered the "weekly journal of progress.")*

The following complementary notice of Red Bluff, some of her citizens, the business outlook, etc., we clip from the San Francisco Elevator of June 5th.

At 4 o'clock P.M. Sunday, we left Wheatland for Red Bluff, where we arrived in four hours after a pleasant ride in the cars through a rich farming country, luxuriant with teeming grain. This beautiful inland city is at the head of navigation about two hundred and twenty-five miles from San Francisco. It is the county seat of Tehama County and beautifully situated in the Sacramento Valley and surrounded by extensive farms. Tehama county is also famous for its flocks and herds. Not seeing any person I knew, I got in the "bus" belonging to the Tremont Hotel kept by J. W. Burgess, on main street. The Red Bluffians are fond of good living, if the hotels and good eating houses are evidence: the accommodations are first-class, the meals excellent, the host obliging and charges reasonable. After lunch I inquired the way to Mr. Delvecchio's and a friend (I really forgot his name) very obligingly conducted me to his residence. I accompanied the family to the M. E. Church where the Centennial celebration of the organization of Sunday Schools in Glouster, England, was in progress of which we give a notice in another column, copied from the People's Cause on Monday evening. An evidence of the prosperity of Red Bluff is seen in the fact that they support two daily papers – the People's Cause and Daily Sentinel. The former is published every evening by J. H. Pryor; it is Republican in politics and is ably conducted. The latter is an evening paper of Democratic proclivities. I believe both are well supported.

There are three colored barbers; Messrs. C. Delvecchio, C. E. Christian and Jas. Logan, all, I believe, are doing a profitable business. There are other colored mechanics in Red Bluff, but I only became acquainted with one, Charles Graffell, a blacksmith. Allen Coffee [sic Alvin Coffey], an extensive farmer who lives at Elder Creek, about twelve miles from Red Bluff, was in town and reminded me of an unfilled promise to visit his farm and I willingly complied and will notice the jaunt in my next.

Weekly People's Cause, June 19, 1880:

Tehama County's Colored Citizens —The editor of the Elevator, San Francisco, spent a few days in Red Bluff some time since and

for the benefit of our colored people we give in full his second
letter descriptive of his trip to the county, favorable mention of
individuals, etc. It will be read with interest by all.

In my last I mentioned a contemplated visit to Elder Creek, the
residence of Mr. Alvan [*sic* Alvin] A. Coffey. This is about twelve
miles from Red Bluff, which we left at about 8 o'clock p.m. riding
through a richly cultivated country. We were accompanied by
Messrs. Griffin Logan, stock-raiser and Peter Hubbard a farmer. I
was delighted with the ride. To me it was a realization of county life
more than I had ever before seen. After leaving Red Bluff we rode
several miles without seeing a house or any sign of inhabitants.
When I rewarded to my companions the absence of houses they
laughed heartily at my ignorance of rural life, and asked me how
I would have liked to have crossed the plains in the early days of
California, when they didn't see a hut, nor tent, nor any sign of
human life for weeks. Good company, and a pleasant star-light
evening made the ride seem short. We left Mr. Hubbard at his
residence and in less than three hours arrived at Mr. Coffey's farm,
where I was cordially welcomed by Mrs. Coffey and the whole
family. Mr. Coffey has seven children, only three of whom are on
the ranch, two sons and a daughter. One of his sons is married, and
I believe also a daughter. The youngest son, Alvan [Alvin] Coffey,
Jr. is a mechanic and resided in Red Bluff. The elder sons reside
on their own farms. Mrs. and Mrs. Coffey were originally slaves in
Missouri, of which they are not ashamed, as many of our own race
are. By his own industry he purchased himself, his wife, and his
oldest children, and is now in good circumstances, owning a large
farm, and enjoying an amiable reputation for integrity and business
capacity. He has given his children good examples, and such
education as the country schools afford. I remained at Mr. Coffey's
until Wednesday, when I returned to town, accompanied by Mr.
and Mrs. Griffin Logan and two of their children.

Our ride to Red Bluff was as pleasant as our ride out. Mr.
Logan, who is well acquainted with the country, directed our
attention to points of interest. East of us was the Sierra Mountains
covered with snow. In front, and almost due north, old Shasta rears
his hoary head. This is truly the Monarch of Mountains, crowned
with a diadem of eternal snow, and a snowy mantle envelopes
his huge gray form from base to summit. This is a grand sight. It
was continually in view, shifting occasionally from left to right,

according to the sinuosities of our road, but generally due north. The Butte range, of which Mount Shasta is the terminus extends west, and is lost in the Coast Range.

After our arrival at Red Bluff, I visited several of our friends in that pleasant city. Mr. Charles H. Delvecchio owns half a block on one of the principal streets. He has erected several neat cottages which rent to good advantage. Mr. W. R. Robinson has a beautiful residence on Jefferson Street. Mr. Robinson has two amiable daughters, Miss Clara Logan and Miss Laura Robinson. His son, Mr. James Logan, who was married a few months ago, has gone to house keeping. Mrs. Pauline Logan, has a fine residence a couple of blocks from her sister, Mrs. Robinson.

The colored residents of Tehama County are generally in a prosperous condition. Sandy Baulch [sic Balch], whom I met in Red Bluff, is a substantial farmer as is also his son J. L. Baulch [Balch]. I will also notice Messrs. Geo. Homan [sic Holman], Richard Trotter, Virgil Dixon and other colored men have fine farms.

The colored school on Oat Creek, a short distance from Mr. Coffey's, was formerly taught by Miss Clara Logan. Last session it was in charge of Miss Sarah Sanderson, who gave entire satisfaction. The trustees of this school are Messrs. A. A. Coffey, James Holman and Moses Soloman [sic Solomon]. It is rumored that our agent Charley Christian has captured the young school Marm, if so, Oat Creek School will require another teacher next session.

We cannot mention all the friends we saw in Red Bluff but we will mention a few whose names we remember; the omitted will excuse us. Messrs. D. O. Bryant, formerly of San Jose, H. L. Scott, Elias Twine and Horatio Scott formerly of Oakland. Thursday morning we left Red Bluff after as pleasant a visit as we ever made. ◉

Source

Black Pioneers of Tehama County (available at TehamaCountyHistory.com)

Douglas Cone brought the first purebred Herefords to Tehama County when he purchased 55 head for $8,000 from Governor John Sparks of Nevada (ca. 1899). "Horned Herefords" were once the most popular bulls in Tehama County and his Berendos herd was famous. White-faced cattle were such a curiosity that a gentle three-year-old bull named Aaron was kept at the Freeman Stable in Red Bluff for a week to be admired in January 1900 (Tehama County Library archives).

Early Los Molinos and Manton Memories

Carl Anton Meyer[1]

Can't you imagine how wonderful it must've looked in the early days, with the elk, the deer, even a few grizzly bears and the wildcats, puma, what have you? In this area, there must've been all awful lot of them including the Indians that lived along the Sacramento River. I've been helping my brother-in-law at his place; there must be three or four acres where the ground is very soft and dark from the campfires. It's an awful place if you

---

1 These memories are compiled from three tapes Carl did in 1980 when he was 79 years old. Unlike more formal settings with an interviewer, a set of questions, and the interviewee, these are individual conversations he had recorded when the mood hit, and he talked about anything that came to mind. This transcript maintains his voice and opinions (he earned them), with only minor edits made when necessary for clarity.

Carl was born in Oakland, California, in 1901. His father, John D. Meyer, was born in Germany and came to California in 1880 when he was 16. Carl's mother was also born in Germany; her father's name was Karl Leitoff. She lived in England after her father died. Her grandfather, a sea captain, lost his ship in a storm in the North Sea and that's how she ended up living in England. She later emigrated to the Bay Area.

After Carl's parents married, they settled in Tehama County in 1908. Carl's siblings were John, Ludwig (also known as Louis), Herman, Freda, Clara, and Katy. —JRS, *Editor*

have to work the grounds because it's all powdery, and it comes up in your face, making you look like the dickens when night comes. It's where the Indians used to fish and hunt. The Sacramento River in them days, lots of salmon came up the river. I date here from 1908 in Tehama County; came up from Oakland as a boy. But there used to be a lot of salmon even in my time and more in the early days, must have had a pretty good time of it, hunting and everything.

In my opinion, this is one of the richest grazing grounds in the United States. The streams cutting across it from the mountains; oaks that were all through the Sacramento Valley. In my day when I was a youngster, there must've been millions and millions of oak trees; every three or four acres had oak trees, and they were large. I've seen oak trees, I imagine, up to about seven feet through. What we call swamp oak, some call them Valley Oak— they really are not quite so handsome, but they are magnificent trees.

As I recollect these things, I'm not one of your historians, I'm just a story-teller. I try to tell a true story, and if I make any mistake in my storytelling, I'm sorry because I consider them true, and I'm pretty good at that. If you don't like it and want to accuse me of being a liar, you may, even though you may get a good punch in the nose.

Joseph Cone

Joe Cone bought the Rancho de los Berrendos, a Mexican land grant, and another grant above Los Molino's. Joe Cone, like Stanford, was a very progressive man and a good banker. He built a rock fence along the east side of his valley land. If you go along 99E, you'll see it off to the right-hand side. It's been there, some say, about 100 years, but this is a guess on my part.

Cone sheep, 1905 (Tehama County Library archives)

My brother's father-in-law, Taylor, was foreman over the Chinese. They made 17 cents a day building a sturdy rock fence by hand. You can see that rock fence for miles away. It extends down to about Los Molinos. It was to keep the range cattle out of the valley. [2]

He had lots of sheep in there, too, from Salt Creek down to and beyond Los Molinos. Cone had about 20,000 head of sheep or more. He had summer ranges in the mountains. Old Sam Childs (my brother's father-in-law) tells me it was about 100 miles from his home ranch up to where he had the summer range. He also had close to about 100 head of cattle. He had about 100 head of mules that did his work, and they certainly were fine mules.

On Antelope Creek, he built an electric light plant and ran his electricity to Red Bluff. He also built on his ranch an ice plant in the early days, the Cone Ice Company.

On the Cone ranch was the largest pear orchard for many years, largest in California or the United States, I don't know which. When they went to pull them out after they were about 70 or 80 years old, they had an awful time of it. Cone also had quite a large prune orchard.

---

2 In the years 1880-1882, Joseph Cone brought a large number of Chinese to Red Bluff to build rock walls on his acreage. These have been a curiosity of Tehama County since their construction, which spans approximately 40 miles. Cone hired as many as 100 Chinese at a time secured by a contract with the Tongs in San Francisco.

The walls were built so Cone, who turned his sheep loose in the foothills in the wintertime without supervision, could keep the various bands separated and to fence them out of the grain fields. The walls are marvels of construction starting with a broad base of huge boulders and pyramiding to as much as eight foot heights of smaller stone without the use of any kind of mortar. The rocks were so cleverly sized and fitted by the Chinese stone masons that most of the construction is as solid today as when it was erected 130 years ago.

The Chinese were paid 15 cents a rod (16.5 feet). Cone furnished the horses, stone boats, and cradles. The cradles were large, open topped wooden boxes fitted with two long handles extending front and back on two sides. They were filled with small rocks, and depending on the weight, carried by four or eight Chinese to the site of the fence and dumped where the stone masons applied their craft. The stone boats were much larger than the cradles and were used to move the big rocks, pulled by teams of horses. It is hard to imagine how many thousands of rattlesnakes the Chinese uncovered while building the rock walls, not to mention how they suffered from snake bites throughout the construction. These walls serve as a lasting tribute to Cone and his Chinese laborers. There is absolutely no truth to the rumor that Cone murdered his Chinese laborers and buried their bodies in the rock fences. (Cheryl Conard Haase, "The Remarkable Life of Joseph Spencer Cone," 2016 TCGHS Memories).

On this ranch, he had places with barns every so often. There was one at his home ranch, right below Dye Creek, then down below that, there was another one, and one down below that yet. As they went down country plowing, they'd have these places where they fit their mules and kept the people while working. They were great big barns, although, the barns were smaller at the home ranch.

In about 1870, Sam tells me, a large barn burned up, and Cone lost all his working stock. He went up to Modoc and bought lots of wild horses and mules. Sam says they had to buck horses every day when they were working with those. Modoc horses and mules were noted for their own orneriness. Sam said he built a number of barns. One was a brick barn, and then he had three or four other barns, maybe more than that. But generally, he had about two large barns to store hay in.

Cone owned 50 percent of Cone-Wards sheep outfit east of Los Molinos. They ran about 18,000 to 20,000 head of sheep. The interesting thing about that was that Ward and Cone were friends, but they had an arrangement that whoever had a son first would get a 51 percent stake. Douglas Cone was born before any of the Wards, so Cone got the 51 percent. But Doug never amounted to much. When he grew up, he used to go to Red Bluff every night to gamble or drink. His dad was very unhappy with that, and he used to make Doug work every day out in the fields with the men. But Doug had his own horse and buggy, and he would ride to town every night.

Los Molinos Land Company

When Joseph Cone passed away, his wife and three children subdivided the ranch and parts were developed into the Los Molino's Land Company.

Panorama of Los Molinos facing east. The dirt road will eventually become Hwy 99E. The large structure is the Los Molinos Inn, which is now the empty lot (Tehama County Library archives).

There were a lot of mosquitoes and everything. They didn't have mosquito abatement like now. The land wasn't leveled, and there were places where water stood. Los Molinos Colony had quite a name for having lots of malaria.

People who were savvy and had a little money could make a go of it. They worked hard for land colonization. But others didn't make it. Lots of hard work and lots of grief there. But I guess it was worth it.

Father came through here in 1884 to go to Whitmore, Shasta County. In those days, it was just a dirt road right through the Cone Ranch. This road was built in 1884. Hardest place to get started was in Los Molinos because they had to cut big 6-foot pine trees down to get the land cleared.

It was very new in 1918 when it was built. I was there and watched it, but I didn't get to work on the road that came by our house. They did it mostly with teams. There was an old oil-pulled tractor; it was a one-cylinder. I don't remember the name right now. It ran on coal oil or diesel oil and had a great high drive. It was nothing like a modern tractor. It weighed 11,000 pounds, I'm not sure, and they used that to grade the road out front. The road was gravel and used to wind around towards Los Molinos.

There was an electric railroad that ran from Sacramento to Chico. They expected to run through Los Molinos Colony and make a lot of money. They had a right of way, but they gave it up. So you see, there was no means of transportation except horses, wagons, or buggies or what have you, and sometimes that took quite a while. These pictures look very nice in the movies when they go galloping off on horses in Western attire, but that's not real life.

I lived there for a good many years in the colony. Probably one of the best places to raise peaches in the state, and prunes do awfully well there too. And also, almonds, although they have to be smudged sometimes; it gets a little colder than it does around Merced. There were a lot of dairies in the Los Molinos Colony, but they've got away from that.

The upper part of Cone Ranch stayed in the hands of Doug Cone and his widow [Marie Louise Madeline Lewis Cone]. She ran it for good many years. She had a superintendent, and they had a sheep farm and ran about 20,000 head of sheep, and in the early days about 700 head of cattle.

They raised grain on their land. They didn't take the oak trees out, as I understand it, because there was a lower tax rate in what they could call forest lands. There were enough oak trees that they didn't have to pay such high taxes.

Cone Ranch used to plow their land with low-lying teams; six or eight teams hitched onto these plows and handled the jerk line. That is, only one rope runs up to the leaders and they're told where to go by the "gee" for the one side and the "haw" for the other side. They can be handled very easily that way.

Harvesting grain on the Cone Ranch, 1910 (Tehama County Library archives).

When it came time to haul grain to town, I've often seen them go up the road with a long-line team: six or eight mules hitched to a couple of wagons. They were an interesting sight. When I lived in Red Bluff one summer about 1916 or 1917 or so, I saw these teams—six, seven, eight, or so with wagons. They go to the Willard Mill on the railroad track to unload there or at Fisher's or Cone and Kimball's warehouse.

When the big combines came in, the Cone Ranch used to have a place for horses. I don't know how many. It took 50 or more horses to pull one of them. They were big outfits. Then the Cones bought a traction engine. They were the engines that ran on big drive wheels. I don't know how high the back wheels were, but I would guess eight or nine feet high and the front ones were lower. It was a straw burner; they would throw straw in there. Every so often, some of these sparks would get away, and they'd have a fire out there in the grain field. Later on, the big old Cats [Caterpillar tractors] pulled them.

They did their plowing with teams. During the day, you couldn't get very much work done with a team of horses in the summertime because it was too hot, and in the evening and morning, you had to milk. It was a very hard life. They also had cows and dairies. That's where Dairyville got its name. There are a few modern dairies, but mostly it's peaches, prunes, almonds, corn, beans, and pasture for quite a few cattle.

Cone Ranch was reputed to have 100,000 acres. Lots of these ranches had a lot of river bottomland along with the poor land.

Marie Louise Madeline Lewis Cone

Douglas Cone died relatively young in 1905, leaving his wife, Lou, to run manage everything. He also left her in debt, and these men demanded payment of, but there was a clause in there "in gold coin in US equivalent." She wanted to pay it off. She offered them the check, but they wouldn't accept it. They said it had to be a certain day, and it had to be in gold. So Wells Fargo got the gold. It came into Red Bluff on the train and was unloaded onto a wagon. The sacks of gold were hauled to the bank. Then it got there, and they didn't want to accept it, but they had to. After they did, they were worried because they might get held up. That's a kinda interesting episode. You don't have to take my word for it. There are records of it somewhere in Red Bluff. It was one of the largest shipments that ever came into Red Bluff by Wells Fargo. A true story of the Cone Ranch.

Looking directly at the camera is Marie Louise Madeline Cone sitting next to her husband Douglas Cone on the porch. Behind them is Addie Hughes, T.H. Ramsey, and Mrs. Ramsey (c., 1900) (Tehama County Library archives).

The Indomitable Mrs. Cone

Joseph Cone arrived in California in 1850 with a pony and a mule but died a wealthy man. After passing in 1894, his estate, including the large 100,000-acre Cone Ranch [valued up to $2 million or $73.4 million in today's dollars], was divided between his wife Anna, two daughters (Josephine and Mary), and son, Douglas Spencer Cone, who inherited the northern third of the Cone ranch property, which was valued at a substantial $18+ million in today's dollars. Josephine was married to a land developer J.D. Sherwood, who started the Los Molinos Land Company in 1905 and subdivided the land for settlement patterned after the Maywood Colony in the Corning area.

Douglas blew through his inheritance in 11 years. At his death in 1905 from pneumonia, his estate was only valued at $10,000 ($359,000 in today's dollars), which he bequeathed to his sisters, mother, and wife. However, he was indebted to the Kraft Company Bank in Red Bluff to the tune of $12 million in today's dollars. The bank moved to foreclose on the properties and stock he had pledged as collateral, including the home ranch, Cone & Kimball Company, Bank of Tehama County (Joseph Cone co-founded this bank, and Douglas had been its President), Cone & Ward Company, and the Cone Ice & Refrigerating Company. But they didn't reckon on the gritty determination of his widow, Marie Louise "Lou" Madeline Cone. Questioning the amount demanded, and with a day to spare, she stopped the foreclosure sale set for January 13, 1911, to demand an accounting of the actual debt. After hearing testimony and reviewing the records, Superior Court Judge Ellison's ruling on April 12, 1911, gave her 75 days to settle the $364,922.88 debt.

Banks were willing to buy the ranch from her instead of loaning her money to satisfy the debt. Even her wealthy Bay Area family refused to help. Eventually, with the aid of E. F. May of San Francisco, she secured a loan from the German Savings and Loan Association to settle the debt. When she presented a cashier's check to the Kraft Company Bank in Red Bluff, they refused it, telling her, "Your note calls for gold coin, and we want United States gold coin." She returned to San Francisco to exchange the cashier's check for gold. Accompanied by three shotgun-toting guards, she and 20 bags filled with $20 gold coins traveled back to Red Bluff on Train No. 16. The coin weighed 1,500 pounds and cost $500 to transport.

The day before the court-imposed deadline, she walked into the Kraft Bank with the gold coin. Incredibly, they refused to accept her payment. Their reason? They didn't have a place to keep it, so she would have to bring the gold back to San Francisco where it could be deposited in a more secure bank, which would conveniently make her miss the payment deadline. As related by Judge Wetter in 1981 when he told this story, "Knowing Lou Cone, I imagine she had a word or two to say about that. She could be expressive." After very heated discussions, the bank reluctantly accepted the payment and arranged its transport back to San Francisco at a cost of $600.

Lou was a lively, amusing, somewhat eccentric lady with flaming red hair. She could often be seen skipping and exclaiming, "the cherries are ripe," which meant something only to her. Once during her money woes, she was having dinner with a banker who asked if he could remove his coat. She cheekily replied, "I don't care if you remove your pants if you give me the money!" ⊚

The cookhouse of the bunkhouse was run by Chinamen. She always had Chinese helpers working there. She had a superintendent who had a few drinks too many, and he tried to tell the Chinese chef what to do. So he went in there and started telling him where to get off. The Chinese grabbed a meat cleaver and chased him out. He went to Mrs. Cone who told him to stay out of that bunkhouse; he could have the say over the ranch but not over the bunkhouse.

During the depression, Mrs. Cone wanted to fix the house up. She got a loan for $40,000 and put it all into that house. They were kind of hard up in those years. One time, after World War I, she wanted more money for her wool. She held it for a couple of years, and then, finally, she had to sell it for a lot less he could have got before. She lost thousands and thousands of dollars.

Manton

Hogs

When I came to Manton about 1908, we had lots of hogs. Everybody had lots of hogs including farmers and stockman. Acorns can kill cattle, but the hogs ate the acorns and kept them from bothering the cattle.

The hogs enjoyed eating rattlesnakes. It was easy for a hog to kill a rattlesnake if it was a good size. I've seen them kill snakes. It didn't take long for them to finish up. They had a very enjoyable time eating them. We also had lots of coyotes, foxes, and lynx in those days, but we didn't have so many ground squirrels. The coyotes kept them down to a certain extent.

Dad didn't like the hogs when he bought the place. He butchered them all. He had a pretty good butchering place in smokehouse and everything. These hogs ran wild. They were vicious sometimes. They would just as soon bite you at you as look at you seems like.

We had different ways of getting the hogs to town. I'd heard of them being driven to Red Bluff, Cottonwood, or Anderson. We hauled them. It was 32 miles to Red Bluff, but we had to haul them at night. We loaded them when it got dark, and we didn't have any loading chutes. The driver had to drive all night. Sometimes, the moon went down, and the road was narrow with big rocks. It was not a very wide road. It took a lot of close looking to stay on that road. You drove all night to get to the butcher in town. One of them was Vestal. He had a butcher shop on Walnut Street and butchered his own meat. He was one of the best butchers, very clean about it.

In the winter, we would haul them in the daytime if it was cool enough, and in the summertime, at night. As you know, hogs die very easily when they get overheated.

Hogs get very dangerous. I remember when I was a little bit older, I chased hogs out of the alfalfa. I used to have a dog. He was a good hog dog and pretty smart, but sometimes he let his guard down. I remember a time when the hogs circled around back of him, 30 or 40 of them, they closed him in. But the dog would hump on their backs when they were snapping at them with their big mouths. If you've ever seen hogs eat black walnuts or peach pits, even a dog has no comparable bite to them. And he'd run right over them from where he had been encircled.

Other times, I carried a club about two or three feet long and waded into the hogs to give my dog a path out. More than once, those hogs turned on me and tried to bite me. But I was young and strong in those days and pretty good at knocking them at the end of their nose, right on the snout. Hogs are tough if you hit them on the head or the shoulders, but if you hit them right on the end of the nose with a good hearty stick, that hog is going out of business for a while because it hurts. Those were interesting days.

When we walked to school there was a big wild boar. Oh, he was a big fellow with a tusk sticking out of the side of his nose. He'd be standing right close to a path where we had to cross the company ditch on a foot plank, quite a large ditch below Manton. And, by golly, there was this hog standing about 20 feet away. He's chomping his teeth, foam dripping out of his mouth; he sure looked mean. We were a lot happier after we got over that ditch. We didn't know what he would do—charge us? That hog must have weighed 400 pounds, I guess. He was mean and was an old fellow.

A man by the name of Johnson at the upper end of Bend went to chase a boar one time. The boar charged him, and Johnson fell over. Right there, the hog would've ripped him open if his dog hadn't charged in and saved his life. These dogs can be quite helpful in a case like that.

Personally, I don't trust the hog, although I have a lot of respect for their intelligence. I had a pet Brookshire sow one year that I was very fond of. She was so intelligent she seemed to think a lot of me. I couldn't afford to keep her, and I felt bad when I sold her to the butcher. That's the only hog I ever felt really bad about.

My Dad used to raise all kinds of stuff: carrots, beets, potatoes. I raised beans, apples, prunes, all kinds of stuff. Stuff that wasn't so good, we put in a big vat and mixed the stuff together. Then we mixed in some bran that Dad bought for 99 cents a sack, lit a fire under it, and boiled that all up. We fed the hogs with that at night; they sure did well on it. That was in the wintertime, and in the summertime, they ran out in the pasture with quite a lot of woods. They did quite well without feed except swill.

We used coal oil in the house. We had no gas or electricity in those days. After we used the 10-gallon can, we cut the top out of it and put a handle on it with heavy hop wire. We use these to carry the stuff out to the hogs. All food scraps went in those cans. We had a cow, so if there was a little extra milk, we added it.

They sure did relish that stuff. In the evening, we'd call them in, and they'd come running for half a mile away sometime. When they all got there, we'd dump these big cans into long troughs, and you should have seen those hogs gobble. One time, when I was feeding them, three white Chester hogs, a boar and two young sows, stood face-to-face and started singing. It was better than lots of opera I've heard. They had very clear, high voices. The two young ladies sang soprano, and the male sang high tenor. Some of the nicest music I've ever heard, although I couldn't understand what it meant.

There was one time when we butchered a hog that didn't belong to us. It was a small one and was running with wild ones. Somebody had marked it, but Louis went up and inquired around as to whose mark that was. Nobody knew. It was running wild in his place. So he didn't know what to do. In them days, things were different. We lived a long ways from town and could have spent years trying to find out whose mark that was. I don't know if they had brand or earmark books in them days. We hunted this hog down. He was only a small hog, about two years old, about 200 pounds, and I don't think he dressed out to about 50 or 60 pounds of meat. I was scared that someone would come along and catch us butchering an earmarked hog. Louie and Dad laughed at me, but I can't think they liked it themselves. We butchered it, and when we got all done, Louis took the ears and cut them all up so nobody could tell whose mark that was.

Early Schools

Not quite a mile south and a little bit to the east of Manton was a very early-day school. It was not even on a county road. It was a school before the regular roads were laid out. I think the Hazens and a few others went there to school. It was small, and I never saw the school in operation. I was told about it by a woman, an early settler, but I never saw the school. I just saw some of the wood lying around there and saw the lava rock that was squared off for the foundation. Those days, they didn't use any concrete or anything; they just used lava rock—find some flat lava rock and put the beams on it.

Later on, when people got to settling more in there, there were six schools near Manton; Pinegrove, Benton, Lee, Junction, Rockland (up towards Forwards), Macum Springs (it was on the road from Paynes Creek to Manton, just a little ways where Macum Springs comes out). Later on, that school was moved down to the bottom of Battle Creek, right where you go along at the bottom of the creek. These schools would all have big bells on top of them, and you could hear them ring.

These three schools—Lee, Benton, Pinegrove—could have been in Shasta or Tehama Counties, one, two, or all three. This history I've told about his Manton is Tehama and Shasta Counties together because, to my mind and everybody else up there, we didn't consider the boundary line of Manton to be Digger Creek because that was all Manton country. We felt like we all belonged to Manton, not to either Shasta or Tehama Counties. In those days, Redding and Red Bluff were a long ways off.

Schools were run rather inexpensively. Junction was a large two-room school with an anteroom in front where you washed and put lunch buckets, etc., and then

Manton Junction School (TCGHS archives).

the main room that could hold 40 to 50 pupils. It had a large stove that took about three-foot wood, which was sure needed in the winter. Junction was about three-quarters of a mile south of Manton, right along the South Powerhouse Road, which they used to call Hazens Road. The Hazens were early settlers in that country, and they had a beautiful ranch there with lots of water.

I'm going to tell you about how these schools were operated. They had one teacher, and I think she was paid $70 or $75 a month, but she wasn't paid during the summer vacation. The teacher had all classes from the first to the eighth. For a while there, we had the ninth grade in our grammar school, and she had to do all that work herself. So she would have to take lots of her stuff home at night because, with all those classes, she didn't have time to do them. We went five days a week, if I recollect. The school started at 9 o'clock and ended by four.

We had a janitor, and he got from $2.50 to $3.50 a month, and he had a lot of work to do. He had to get up there, start a fire in the stove, and carry in wood. This was long, heavy wood—about three feet long and fairly thick—about three pieces made a big, heavy arm full or four pieces at the most. They could put two or three pieces in the stove, and boy, you ought to see that stove red-hot lots of times. We sure like to have it sometimes in the wintertime.

Our ditch ran alongside the schoolyard there, which was about two acres. The janitor had to go over there to get a bucket of water, about 2½ gallons of water, and carry it up to the school. He had to sweep and clean and dust all the desks, etc. During the school day, he had to carry in wood and carry out the ashes, and he had to ring the bell at 8:30. The teacher rang the bell at 8:55 for us kids to get ready, and at 9:00, she rang the bell again for us to be in when school opened. We lived about a mile below Manton at a downslope, but I could hear the Junction school bell on ordinary, clear days. It was a beautiful-toned bell. It sits up there today at the joint school in Manton, the same bell I used to ring.

At one time, I was a janitor for month up there. The janitor broke his arm, and I had the chance to have that job. I thought it was pretty nice; I was able to buy 25-20 shells and a few little other things with the money that I made that month, and I sure was happy about that, but I was greatly relieved to get rid of that job; man, there was a lot of work to that. You sure did a lot of work for that little bit of money.

I think we had three trustees, but there might've been four. There was one head trustee, and he was a clerk. He came in and talked expenses every so often over with the teachers, and they were very critical about things. Everything had to be accounted for because the people were poor, and they weren't wasteful. There was not the waste in those schools that there is today. When I first went to school in Manton in the fall of 1908, there were about 40 students, or pupils as we called them, and they ranged up to 20 years; they had first to ninth grade then.

There was some rowdy bunch that went to school that came from Manton, and they just ran the school. They used to jump in and out the windows while the teacher had class and everything else. They used to shoot spitballs at the teacher while she sat at the desk, fixing her papers at recess or noon. They would just stand there and shoot spitballs. There was nothing she could do. I think her name was Ms. Smith. It was generally a mess. She was a small woman and not very offensive, so they weren't very nice and were really rough.

I remember one time it was snowing, and I had to go to the toilet. Our toilets were outside, and I came in, and one of these big boys had a snowball that he made out of water and snow. I don't know if you've ever been hit by one. It was large. He was a man already, and he threw it is just as hard as he could at another boy, which missed him and hit me in the side. That sure hurt a long time.

Teaching jobs, especially ones at Manton like Junction School, were very much sought after, because they had a place where they could board in Manton and they didn't have to live way out with farmers. They had it pretty good that way, and they like the school because it was a little bit better than the average country school.

The next year, when it started up in the fall of 1909, we had a new teacher, and she was a horse of a different color. She was young, but fairly tall, and built big enough so she could take it. So, when these big kids showed up to go to school the next year, they had their fun again—it was four or five real rowdy ones. The trustees were there and told them to beat it, that they weren't going to allow it anymore. The trustees were all ranchers. The biggest one there weighed about 240 pounds, and he was constable with his star; they weren't the type of men who gate gave up easily. The troublemakers didn't want no trouble with them, so they went home, and this teacher was hired to handle the class.

At that time, we still had 35 kids going there, so she took up classes and told them what was going to happen. One of the big kids, that is, a seventh or eighth grader, started talking down to her. Pretty soon she dismissed classes and sent one of the kids out for some red buds, which make awfully good whips. Then she locked the doors and she and that big kid had it out. You could hear the whips and him hollering. When she got done with that fellow, who was just as big as she was, he was sitting at his desk, and she was at her desk, but there was no more trouble after that.

There was a happy sequel to it. The Northern California Power Company had a head engineer putting a bunch of tunnels in on South Battle Creek to run to South Powerhouse. This engineer was going with the school teacher, and he resigned that fall. Next spring, they got married. Married teachers were frowned upon because they felt that these young teachers were "starry-eyed" about teaching, and they were going to do some wonders in the world, which they did. They sure helped bring up a lot of nice kids.

We had to walk to school. I had to walk three-quarters of a mile up a pretty steady grade. One night, it snowed. It was still about a foot deep and icy right up to the top from the snow that had melted and then froze during the night. When I went to school that next morning, I was stepping on the snow, and then, boom, down you went right to the bottom, and every step was that way. Boy, my legs were sore, and I was tired when I got to school.

Some years ago, I was quite surprised when my brother told somebody in my presence that we were poor people in those days. I was kinda shocked, because we had a pretty good ranch, and Dad hired two or three people to work for us several times. I thought we were fairly well fixed, but when I look back on it, the way you people have money in everything, we were poor.

We had some neighbors that were not really well fixed. These people were a little poorer than we were, and not that their home was any worse in any way because there was certainly a lot of love in that home. But they were a large family and hard up for money. Their dad had only 480 acres, and he had some cows and a team of horses, and he had a meadow so that he could raise some crops. The boys fished, and in the winter, they trapped mink coyotes, bobcats, lynx, what have you.

Skunks brought a pretty good price in those days for furs, and these boys would trap them. They would come to school in the same clothes that they wore when they skinned the skunks out, and there was a pretty good little odor wafting from them. The teacher never liked that, but she couldn't say too much about it. Things were kind of rough with them, although you wouldn't know it. They were really nice people, honest and hard-working, and I certainly respected them.

When they came to school, I noticed that one or two of them would walk through the snow and brush for about two miles to school. We all had to walk to school. This one boy's shoes were broken in front, and there was a hole in there, and the snow water would run in and out when he was sitting there in school. The teacher always let them sit by the fire; they didn't have to ask; they could just sit by the fire and dry their shoes out. So things were awfully good in some ways, but in other ways, they weren't so good.

I'm going to tell a story now that you can believe or not, but I'm satisfied it's a true story. The woman who told it was there. She was a good, dependable woman. Her name was Paselk, and she was about 50 years old, I think. She and her husband have long since passed on. I don't think that even one of her children are living anymore. I think they have all passed on.

It was about the 1870s or the 1880s, and the country was a wilderness, you might say, at that time. The panthers and bears and stuff were not scared as they are today because they had not been shot at much and hadn't got the fear of human beings.

This little girl was going home from school, and she had two walk two miles through that rough country to get home. There wasn't a road in them days except probably an old road that went by that school. The rest was all wilderness. It was a closed winter; it had been snowing and storming all the time, and the wild animals like bear and panther would come down lower to get out of the snow.

She was walking home. She had one of those old-fashioned lunchboxes. It was one of those tobacco boxes that held either a pound or two of smoking tobacco. It had a handle on top and a lid, and they made awfully good lunchboxes. Anyway, inside of this was a canner jar that her mother had sent something like cooked beans in that kids could eat during lunch while sitting by the woodstove at school.

She noticed something following her. It was a panther. At first, it followed her at a distance. She was 9 years old and all by herself. Pretty soon, the animal got braver. He was hungry. As she walked along, this panther kept getting closer and closer, and finally, it got brave enough to lunge at her. To protect herself, all she had was this lunchbox, so she waved it, and the strange rattling from the canner jar inside it scared the panther, so it backed off. She kept that up until she got within calling distance of her father, and her father came. She didn't run; she just walked. She was a brave little girl. When her father came in sight, she hollered, *"Panther! Panther!"* He came out and shot it with his rifle. In those days, the rifles were all left loaded. I used to leave my loaded years ago. Today, I don't on account of my kids, but them days, those were different kinds of days.

Manton Jail

At Manton, we had the justice of the peace and a constable on our side in Tehama County. I really do believe that these justices of the peace in places like Manton were more effective and impressed the people more with law and order than what high falutin' judges and justices of the peace do when they don't know the people. They knew the people there, and there was generally a good, worthwhile person as justice of the peace and also as constable. They were usually property owners, and they weren't too extravagant. We had a jail up there, too, that was built by the County. There were two rooms. It had no windows in it except right in front: there was an open place with bars and no glass in it. I noticed that when somebody

The Manton jail was built about 1902 from 2 foot x 4 foot fir. Its first inmate was a man jailed for stealing turkeys, Hugh Robertson. After that, it was called Robertson's Fort for a time. It was also used to store black powder. Here, Henry Myer is passing on a sled pulled by mules (c. 1925).

in there, they'd be looking right across the street at the Barnes store, see their friends and other people, and there they were: in jail. It must not have been a very nice feeling to be locked up there. As far as I can recall, I can't recollect anybody being locked up twice because I don't think they exactly enjoyed it.

People would get locked up if they were disorderly, ornery, or something, and the justice of the peace would hand down a sentence. If people got arrested on the Shasta County side, they would be taken over to the Manton jail because it was a long way to Redding. In that way, they didn't have to bother with transporting a prisoner except when he was a prisoner of importance that the Superior Court was to hand down a decision on.

We have a doctor, Dr. Hoyt who got drunk up there. The constable was in a hurry to get back to the dance, and he didn't search for matches. I guess the doctor wanted to see what time it was or something, so he lit some matches and got the jail on fire. Somebody noticed it, and they run down there. It burned quite a little. Years ago, you could see the smudges on the inside; they gradually disappeared, though. Hoyt was in such bad shape that he couldn't talk for a number of days; he very nearly got burned up. Being a small fire, they were able to put it out using buckets; that's the only fire I have seen put out with buckets. Bramlett Ditch was across the road,

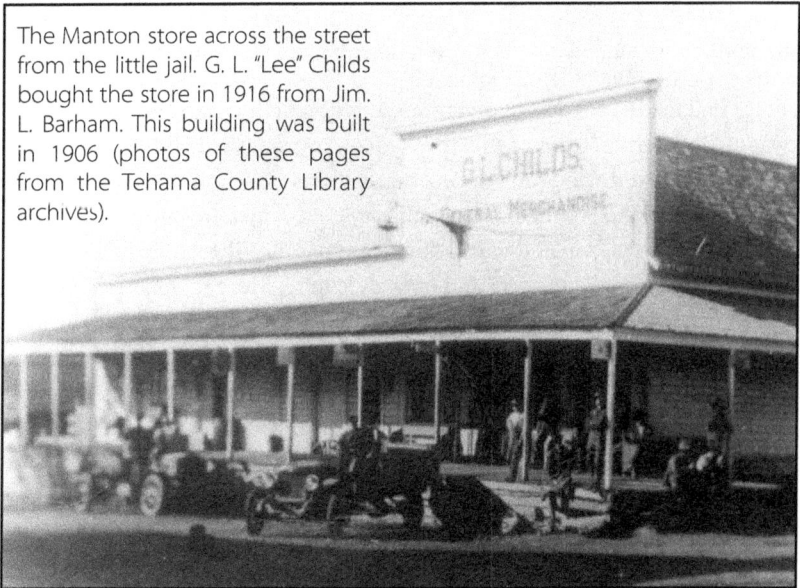

The Manton store across the street from the little jail. G. L. "Lee" Childs bought the store in 1916 from Jim. L. Barham. This building was built in 1906 (photos of these pages from the Tehama County Library archives).

and they carried water from it in buckets to the fire. They very nearly killed this doctor. Now, he wasn't so bad, but the constable wanted to show off what an important guy he was, so he arrested him and put him in jail for drunkenness. He wasn't really bothering anybody, and the people were rather indignant about him being locked up.

Teams and Wagons

Teamsters were hardy characters because they had quite a bit invested in their horses and wagons, which weren't cheap them days. Straight wagons were big affairs; they held tons of freight. The Manton Road would be dust five inches deep in the summertime and bedrock during the winter. Right below Dale's was one of the bad places. The road must've been 200 feet wide, and you'd see those deep ruts. Once in a while, you'd see a post stuck up in there: they'd swipe a post from a fence to help them get out of there. A lot of times, they'd stand the post on and to let people know it was probably too deep to cross. There were no header wagons like you see around nowadays or even a lot of the overland wagons like you see in TV movies; they were nothing but header wagons.

Once they were hauling dynamite to a camp because the Northern California Power Company needed to clear out rocks for tunnels and ditches. They were doing a lot of dynamiting. Bill Bates had three big wagons and ten horses going along what they called a road then (where they rolled the biggest rocks out, the loose ones, and let the rest stay). You can imagine how rough that was if you've ever been back in that country.

Bates had loaded solid with dynamite, and one of the boxes rolled off the wagon, fell right in front of the front wheel, and smashed all the pieces. But the dynamite didn't go off. For one thing, it was frozen [nitroglycerin freezes at about 52°F and is very stable when very cold or frozen], and also, it was new dynamite, although it was industrial dynamite. There was a difference between industrial dynamite and farm dynamite. I forgot what the percentage was, but the percentage was about 20% more nitroglycerin. They used to mix sawdust in the nitroglycerin—that's what's in the old-fashioned sticks of dynamite. If it unfroze ("sweated"), the nitroglycerin would melt and become dangerous to handle. Anyway, he didn't blow up, and he was at our place years later when we heard about it. Dad asked him, and he told us all about it—the box smashed all to pieces, but the dynamite never went off. He had a very reverent way of talking about that, and he ended up saying,

"If that had gone off, why, me and the mules would've been blowed all the pieces." So that was life in the long-line teams.

As you doubtlessly know, the long-line team, or jerk-line team as it was called, was a string of horses or mules strung out 2 x 2 and pulling a wagon. The driver of the jerk line, or mule skinner as he was called, would sit on the right-hand side, and if he was a swamper, he'd sit on the left-hand side. The driver would talk to his horses if he wanted them to turn to the right or the left: it would be "gee" or "haw." He would also control them with his jerk line; it was just one line running to the leaders, and that was generally a heavy strap or rope. They rode the horses. The wheelers were generally big, heavy horses, and the others were not so large. The wheelers could help hold the wagons back a little bit. They had long strips running from these different wagons, sometimes up to three wagons. If they had three wagons, the swamper would pull on two brakes, and the driver would pull on one brake.

The wagon boxes were deep and big. They were about four feet high to hold the stuff in. Those roads were very, very rough in them days, and you just couldn't tie the stuff enough to hold it. The swamper's job was to help take care of the mules and to load and unload these wagons. It was a lot of work to unload these big wagons. I think some of them hauled pretty close to a ton to a horse, and that was a lot of freight; ordinarily, they put two tons to two horses. Sometimes, the jerk line team, when they come to a bad hill, they'd either double up or drop one wagon and pull them up to the top of the hill. There's one or two hills to Manton that were that way.

They may go just as far as Dale Station. He was a stopping place, and he fed the people and the horses. Sometimes, if things weren't going quite right, they'd only make it to Long's and then to Manton the next day. Lots and lots of teams went over that road—long-line teams, two-horse teams, and four-horse teams. And then, of course, you had the buggies.

Livestock Drives

The plains weren't fenced at all up to within four miles of Manton, so the sheep or cattle went through, and they could eat as they went along. Of course, that had to come to an end once that was fenced.

The last band of cattle of any size that went through there belonged to Roy Owens, and they were going up to MacArthur Swamps. I think there were about 840 head of cattle in that band; that's a pretty good-sized bunch of cattle for Manton country. He said he wouldn't do it again because of the fences. He had to rent pasture at my brother's place and keep his cattle over a couple of days, so they didn't lose too much weight. I never saw any cattle of any size going through there after that.

Apples

The power company hadn't really done the Manton country any good. If it wasn't for them, you'd find lots and lots of farms and ranches up there. Hundreds and hundreds of tons of apples were brought down to Red Bluff from Manton. We had a four-horse team, and sometimes, we'd deliver over two tons of apples at least in a load in the fall months. Lots of stores like Pine or Fisher or Cone & Kimball would take a whole load at one time. We also delivered apples to the Cone Ranch.

My brother Louie hauled 2 ¼ tons of beans to Anderson over the Springs Branch Road. He was going along, and although we had a high-wheeled wagon, he mired down in the mud so deep that he had to unload that load and carry it maybe 100 feet or more through the mud and then throw it all in a pile and then drive his team through after he fixed up the double trees and some of the traces with barbed wire and fence post. Then he had to load all those beans up again. Imagine walking through a real muddy place with a 100 pounds of beans on your back and then to throw them up on a real high wagon with high sides on it—throw it up as high as his shoulders anyway. Then, adjust them in the wagon after they're thrown up there. That was a lot of hard work, but that's the way the roads were in them days.

About 1909 or 1910, my Dad built a dryer up there. It was just a hot air dryer; it had great big drums underneath, and a long, wood-burning stove about five feet long. We'd throw wood in there and dry our apples that way. Then we'd haul them to Redding. They generally didn't take too much; they'd only want about a ton and quarter load (they'd use them those days up in the mines above Redding). There were a lot of mines them days and the cooks liked to use dried apples because they were easy to haul, and they could use them in pies, and applesauce, and stuff like that. We made quite a lot of money.

My brothers and sisters and I used to go up there in the evening after school. By lantern light, we used to sit up there in that building and peel apples. We had two big peelers that did practically everything. Then we laid them out on a tray, put them in this dryer, and lit it up. We didn't watch TV or anything else. There is nothing like that, not even radio or anything. We didn't mind doing that too much. We loved our mother and father very much. We were deeply in debt; the fellow bragged that he would get the ranch back but he never did. That's the way things were them days.

At first, my Dad used to go up there and peel apples, but we could talk them out of it; we got more pleasure doing the work and having him stay in the warm house. It's a little bit on the chilly side up there in Manton. A little more chilly than it gets down here. The coldest I've ever known it to be up there was 4°F above zero. Of course, that is awfully cold for some people.

Cars and Roads

Early-days cars were altered cars or roadsters. Among some of the more interesting cars was a steam cart. My brother-in-law had one. It had enough power to go so fast that they never really opened it up. The road wouldn't stand it, and they would have an accident. They hauled a square grand piano on it. They had to take the doors off the car and the legs off the piano and put it crosswise, but they hauled it from Anderson to above Manton in the mountains. It was snowing, but those cars were made to take it. They were built heavy for that sort of thing. That car was a 1923. There is no harm done to the car or piano.

Roy Smith (at Vina, c. 1910) in one of the few cars in Tehama County at that time (TCGHS archives).

My brother bought a Ford 1916, which was an improvement over the ones before. The ones before had carbide lights, but this one had lights from the ignition. If you went in high gear at night, a lot of times, you didn't have much light, and you'd have to put it in low, and if you went in low, you'd have to hold that foot pedal down, which got very tiresome. Those cars were pretty rugged for their day, even if they looked light. They had heavy cast-iron pistons and everything in them that could take a heavy lugging. They had no windshield wiper. The tail light was a coal oil lamp that you had to open up and light every time. If you went over a mud hole, it went out. You had to crank all the cars in them days; they had no battery or anything like that.

The roads were very primitive. If you went up the hill, they had what you call water breaks, which was nothing but a glorified ditch dug sideways across the road from the hill to keep running water off the road. When you went over them, it would sure bust springs and make people unhappy.

DETACHABLE TIRE AND RIM

Most of these cars didn't have demountable (or detachable) rims, so if you had trouble, even if it was the middle of the night or snow or in the summertime when it was way over 100° on those plains there, you had to take your tire off and get the tube out and patch the tube and put the tire back on because we didn't have any demountable rims like we do now.[3]

We didn't have heaters we could turn inside the car on or anything like that. These touring cars and roadsters got pretty cold. You are lucky if you had

---

3 In the early days, a flat tire was changed with the wheel and rim ON THE CAR. Jack it up. Take the tire & inner tube off the wheel. Patch the inner tube. Replace the tire & inner tube. Inflate the tire. Lower the jack.

Demountable rims were a more reliable and less strenuous way to change a flat. Much like today's multiple nuts or bolts wheel system, the demountable rim was held to the wheel by 5 or 6 bolts and clamps. The wheel stays on the car when you change the flat. Just the rim and tire are removed and replaced. (https://michiganmotorcar.com/nuts-bolts-2/shortsville-wheels-detroit-demountable-rims/)

curtains and the isinglass wasn't broken.[4] On a cold morning, it was a job to crank up these cars; they were pretty hard starting. They were good for hauling, though; you sure could haul a lot of stuff, and those fenders were strong; you could tie ten to twelve 1' x 16' foot fence post boards on them.

Cars were generally not used in the wintertime in the early days because they got stuck too easily. There were many spots on the road from Red Bluff to Manton you could get stuck in. In those days, it took a careful, slow driver 3.5 hours; if you went along pretty good, it took 2.5 hours; a real fast driver took 1.5 hours and was apt to break springs, etc., along the way. So, you've got an idea what the roads were like.

Rock Fences Near Manton

Sam Childs used a team to haul rocks to build his fences. Being as there were so many rocks in the field, he thought he might as well build fences when money was kinda short in those days. Rock fences were free.

Sam Childs had come from the East. He was a Union soldier. Later, he punched cows in Colorado, then drove a team in the gold days in Montana. Then he came to California and chopped manzanita wood. He said in those days, manzanita grew all around Red Bluff. In Antelope Valley, he chopped manzanita to sell for firewood. Then he moved to Manton and cleared that land. He built a house and later a hotel. He built a barn, which was a livery stable. He had good water rights; I think he had water rights for 200 inches to his place. He built a ditch up to the creek and the dam, but he was young and husky in those days.

I know of another rock fence that was built by Ben Davis. I think it was built when they put crushed rock on the road. In fact, I think the first rock crusher was wood-burning; it was small and went right up the road. Later, they brought a coal-burning steam rock crusher. It crushed rocks and was stationary. It took the rocks along the fence and used them for the road.

The people who settled in Manton were of all nationalities. Some were Germans, a few French, a few Yankees, and what have you. Some people from Missouri settled along Digger Creek. There were a good many creeks, and they all got water. They would dig ditches to the creek and planted clover and what have you.

---

4 Flexible side curtains with clear celluloid (isingglass) panels that could be attached during bad weather to enclose the interior but still allow people to see out.

Clover

If they were up in the pines, they had to plant red clover to get the best results. It got the pitch out of the land. After you planted red clover, it took something out of the ground and put something in. They had to raise lots of clover for the first couple years. Then, after that, you could raise crops on the land.

When my Dad moved to Manton, he had a stump puller. A horse or two are hitched to a long boom. They go round and round and pull this cable tied to a drum. The cable was generally 1-1/4" plow-steel, so you know they had plenty of power. They were slow, but they could pull a pine tree out or anything else.

We cleared a couple acres, and Dad planted quite a bit with potatoes. This land was full of humus from the manzanitas all through the centuries, and you should have seen the potato crops he got. Boy, those were some of the nicest potatoes I'd ever seen in my life. Northern California Power Company had a thousand men at different camps, and they used a lot of potatoes. That shows you what humus in the land can do; it was some of the best in the country. But if you kept farming, it didn't stand up to long. Some of those grounds, like black adobe, will stand the longest of everything. But sandy ground won't stand very long without using fertilizer. In the early days, Dad raised red clover; then, he could raise other crops, although you could raise beans. The nodules that let off nitrogen from the beans would go into the soil so you could raise beans year after year. Stuff like grain and corn would take the stuff out of the ground and never put it back. They planted a lot of beans, which was a good cash crop. If it was pink beans, it had a tender wine that you could feed to the cattle. You could feed milk cows on that, although they wouldn't give us much milk.

They planted lots of apples in that country. A few planted prunes and cherries. Cherries have done awfully well up there, but there weren't many planted. The two largest cherry trees I ever saw were next to the Hazen house. I never believed that cherry trees could grow that large. The fool that rented the place in later years cut the tops off. If you know anything about cherry trees, you know that's the end of it. The trees died.

Prunes and apples did well. Manton had quite a name for apples in places like Corning and Red Bluff. The volcanic rock and ash had lots of minerals that makes them taste better. Today, the apples you buy are picked green so they'll keep. An apple that won't rot isn't worth eating.

At our place, we had 15 to 20 acres of apples, 12 acres of prunes, and 2 to 3 acres of peaches. Then we had hogs.

Bluetown and the Flume

Blue Ridge Lumber had big mills, and they shipped 2' x 12' lumber down to Red Bluff. This was fine lumber, all the big sugar pine. They shipped lumber from Bluetown. Bluetown was about two miles below Manton. If you go down about two miles, you'll notice a spring and green there. That is where the Blue Ridge Lumber Company was.

There was only one flume from there down, so they had men stationed there to unload this lumber. A good, reliable man I knew told me that there were great stacks of lumber in them days. Some days, all day long, they'd pile lumber, and then when the slack came, they put it back into the flume and send it down. They didn't have a telephone, so they used to telegraph first.

Once in Red Bluff, the lumber was used to make sashes, doors, and everything else there. It was a regular factory and employed quite a few people. Also in the early days, Red Bluff had a factory that made guns, a factory that made brooms, and a factory that made buckskin gloves. There were hunters that give them the deer just to make gloves out of them. What a waste.

Riding the Flume

Vince Wilcox (I'm not talking about young Vince who died as an old man about 10 or 20 years ago; I'm talking about his uncle, Old Vince) had been a justice of the peace (if I recall right), a long-line mule skinner, and he had a ranch there. I certainly treasure his memory. He worked for this company. He used to be a walker on the flume.

You hear a lot about all the people who used to ride; you get the impression that whenever they wanted to go to Red Bluff, they'd hop onto the flume and go. Well, not on that flume, as far as I know. I only know of one man that did and of another man who was sick that was sent down to Red Bluff that way. It was an emergency, and he probably would've died up there, so that was a way to get them down.

But the first man I mentioned thought he'd ride to Red Bluff on the planks, so he got on one and started riding down. Some of these places were fast and really steep. Lumber sometimes got some splinters loose when it came flying down, and one board had a seven- to eight-foot-long splinter on the side of it that stuck right over the flume. When he came down, it ran right through him; he died soon afterward. That's the only one I knew that rode the flume outside the sick man.

Vince told me he never rode the flume because it's too dangerous." Lumber going down these flumes could catch someplace, and the board would get crossways in there. More boards would come down and get caught up, and soon you'd have a bunch of boards piled up. In some places, the water would go pretty fast, coming down there and hitting a bunch of that. Sometimes, you might be 30 or 40 feet off the ground through the canyon. I don't think even the motorcycle daredevils of today would do something like that.

In those days, I think we had more of a will to live. We all, including me, were very active people. We had clean air, good food, good water. It made a good, sturdy people, and we had good thoughts, progressive thoughts. America was a great nation; I don't condone everything its done, but the people were for America and tried to live like people ought to live. We had our drunks—if they drank too much, they didn't last long, or they left the country. It wasn't a country for people who didn't work; it was pretty rough on them.

Northern California Power Company

East of Manton, up in the hills, there used to be quite a settlement in the early days. Must've been 300 or 400 people living up there. They had beautiful places and running water, beautiful climate, better than the valley. But the power companies came along and took all the water. Very few farms up there now. Red Bluff missed a chance at being a large town because of that resort town with all that water they had up there. But when it comes to getting large, it's always been stupid. They chased the railroad out of Red Bluff and never tried to get the college; they could've had it at one time instead of Chico. They had city fathers who always wanted to keep things just so, and they did.

Northern California Power Company came in about 1900, I guess. When we came up to Manton in 1908, they were just putting the finishing touches on the powerhouse and the lines that ran out from the powerhouse and

One of two Best Company stream traction engines used by the Northern California Power Company to haul heavy freight (Library of Congress).

The Empire Flume floated rough-sawn lumber from Lyonsville to Red Bluff.

At the Engebretsen Mill, Billy Glines has a board in the water, and Tony Michelson readies another one, c. 1900. Flume tenders lived along the flume to make sure lumber moved smoothly. A 5-gallon can would be hung from a rope across the flume to rattle when boards passed against it. If the rattling stopped, that usually meant that something was wrong.

Rough-sawn boards floating down the flume. Note the flume tender's walkway next to the flume.

Sierra Lumber Company saw filing room at Lyonsville, c. 1912.

Volta Powerhouse near Manton
(photos on these pages from the Tehama County Library archives).

ditches. It went into operation in 1908—my Dad told me that. I didn't get around there to see it. From the time Northern California Power Company came, there was trouble. They wanted the water.

Here's what that happened to us on the Loggerhead Ditch. My father owned some land where he raised beans. Originally, the Loggerhead Ditch claimed 1,800 inches. The power company got him down to 640 inches. One time, we had an engineer and the ditch man walk up there. They were convinced they weren't getting their share of the water, so they had it measured. Turns out, we were getting 350 inches; the power company stole the rest of it.

We never could win a lawsuit in Shasta County against the Northern California Power Company. Even if they broke standing rules, they'd win. In Tehama County, we could always get our fair justice against any big corporation.

Northern California Power Company was building a ditch, and they were blasting. There was a boy about 11 or so hanging around the man. Well, when they drilled a hole in the rock, and they went to shelter, this boy was with them. And there was a longer than usual time before the blast went off. It was a heavy blast with many sticks of powder. All of a sudden, this boy let out running to the place where the blast was supposed to go off. They couldn't get him and stop him, so when he went off, he was right on top of it, and he got blown—it killed him. His remains must not have been too bad, more concussion than anything. You won't believe, this but this is a true fact. I thought it was a coffin; an old lady up there corrected me and said it was a tank they had him in this. If I recollect right, they had him in alcohol, and they had a glass on top, and you could see this boy. His parents kept him in the parlor.

I know this is a fact because a friend of mine, Henry Sheela, went to their place. They asked my Dad and Henry and I to go in. My Dad didn't, and I didn't either, but Henry Sheela did go in and came out and described to us. He felt very subdued after he came out. Their name was Finley. They lived in Battle Creek bottom, and later on, they moved away.

Women

This story I'm going to tell you now, I'm not going to tell who it is or even his occupation. People are getting funny nowadays, and they're afraid to admit to shooting anybody or their folks shot anybody or anything else. Sometimes, these people need to be shot.

This woman was alone with three little daughters on a ranch with an apple orchard. Her husband was away working in the lumber mill making some money. There were quite a few mills in the hills back of Manton. He was working in the mills. A team of horses was very important to a ranch. If you didn't have horses, you are out of luck. She was quite a few miles out of town. Also, they had no way to make a livelihood. So, he was working away from home because the orchard wasn't in production yet or something. Anyway, she was by herself, and he was at the mills. It was a two-story house. She heard a noise out at the barn. The barn was next to the house. She went out there with a rifle. There was a man leading her horses out of the barn. Well, when he started to go through the gate, she looked down on him and told him, "If you go through that gate with those horses, I'll shoot you!"

He laughed and said, "You don't have gumption enough to shoot me." She shot him through the shoulder. Not that the thief was thought much of, especially that kind of thief. He never stole anything around Manton again. He wasn't shot too bad.

There was a small tribe of Indians near Manton living right below their place. He went down there, and the Indians took care of him till he was cured. That's a true story. The last time I saw her daughter, she didn't want to know anything about it. People are funny nowadays. I think that's why we have so much crime. They don't have the guts to stand up for law and order.

The woman had plenty guts in those days. You think of women's lib in all the women in those days were boss of the household and quite willing to take a chance.

Noble was president of the Northern California Power Company and had a summer home in the mountain. He had some pet deer that he turned loose when he quit. One was a buck who came down to Volta Powerhouse. In them days, there were three or four nice houses for the operators who worked in the powerhouse. There are two operators for each shift, two or three shifts, and a foreman; he was not an operator.

Deer can be dangerous. He had a big rack of antlers and was a mean fellow. He had great sport chasing all the women in the house until he came to Stella's house. Stella was raised in the Manton country. She was a raw-boned young woman, just a bride, and she had a lot of grit. He chased her into the house. She had a teakettle of hot water on the stove as women often did. She grabbed that teakettle and came right out. Deer lunged at her, and when he got close enough, she threw this boiling water over him. This big buck took off and never showed up in that country again. That's the kind of women we had up there in those days.

I know her well. Not only that, but her mother was alone one night with some girls. The chicken coop was a distance from the house. She heard a great commotion, went out with her 30-30 rifle, and started shooting through it. Next thing she heard was loud hollering, "Don't shoot! Don't shoot!" A fellow came out. He told her he was walking through a trail at the back of the chicken house. I never knew there was a trail there, but maybe there was. I don't imagine anybody using that trail too much after that.

Neighbors

The first mail to come up there was carried up from Red Bluff to the old Hazen Ranch. I don't think it ever was a post office.[5] I was told by Sam Childs that there was a big can up there where the people put mail in. As I recollect, that was what Sam Childs told me. He was honest, as most people were up in that country. If the man was a liar or crook, everyone knew it, and there weren't many liars or crooks. Neighbors can be pretty tough with people they don't like. Most people were pretty straight and upright. When you're living with people like that, you'd better be upright too. Life can be pretty hard, especially in them days when they weren't so particular about hurting people's feelings.

Up in that country, when I was a boy, we depended on ourselves a lot. We had no doctor, no hospital. When people got sick, they depended on their neighbors. If they had a doctor, they got the doctor. If not, they called on neighbors. When my mother went to finishing school in England, she learned how to keep house and how to nurse people when they were sick.

Over her life, she's been able to help quite a few people. In this case, our neighbor came about 1.5 miles through the brush from us, two or three miles by road. He came with his buggy to ask mother to come. His son had pneumonia and wasn't expected to live. Pneumonia was very common in

5 It is uncertain how Manton got its name. Many stories abound. One is that the name of "Man's Town" submitted to postal authorities who changed it to "Manton" in 1889. Another is that an early settler, J. M. Meeder, named it after his hometown of Manton, Rhode Island. The area attracted settlers in the 1850s with its productive soil, virgin timber, and creeks supplying water for irrigation and hydropower.

those days. It was called the "old man's friend" because if an older man was feeble and helpless, it would take him out of the misery of this world.

But anyway, she went with him. My mother and the boy's mother worked for 24 hours to save him. They had a hard job on their hands because he was very critical.

The next morning, I went out to our orchard. I went to the back end, and I met my mother coming back. She was so tired; she had to walk through the orchard and timber, but she looked happy. The first thing she said was, "Coy is all right. We saved him."

Have you ever thought how that was? All night, on a ranch a mile and a half from neighbors, those two women, fighting for the boy's life. And it all depended on them. If they've made a mistake, he was gone. There was also a sense of achievement if they made a go of it.

There was a closeness to the families you don't find today. The deepest trials are a little bit remote from us nowadays.

If somebody passed on, there were things that had to be done. The body was prepared for burial. And the neighbors came over. Some made the coffee. Some dug the grave. When the coffin was made, it was generally made by a carpenter or blacksmith or somebody handy with tools. It was generally made of 2-inch planks of cedar if they had it, or red fir. When they got done with that, the women took over. They put sateen or satin in it, black, with pillows, and put the body in there. They stayed in the home one night. What they call a watch. They didn't drink liquor. The strongest they drank was coffee. These were young to middle-aged people who set up all night in respect to the dead person and their relatives. I think there is a little bit more respect for them than there is today. We had no undertakers of the body was not embalmed. They left the coffin open so people could view the remains.

They would get a good wagon, generally a spring wagon, and a good team of horses and haul the body up to the cemetery and have their services there. After about four, five, or ten years, the dirt would begin to sink; then you knew that the remains went back to earth. How much nicer that is, I believe. ⊚

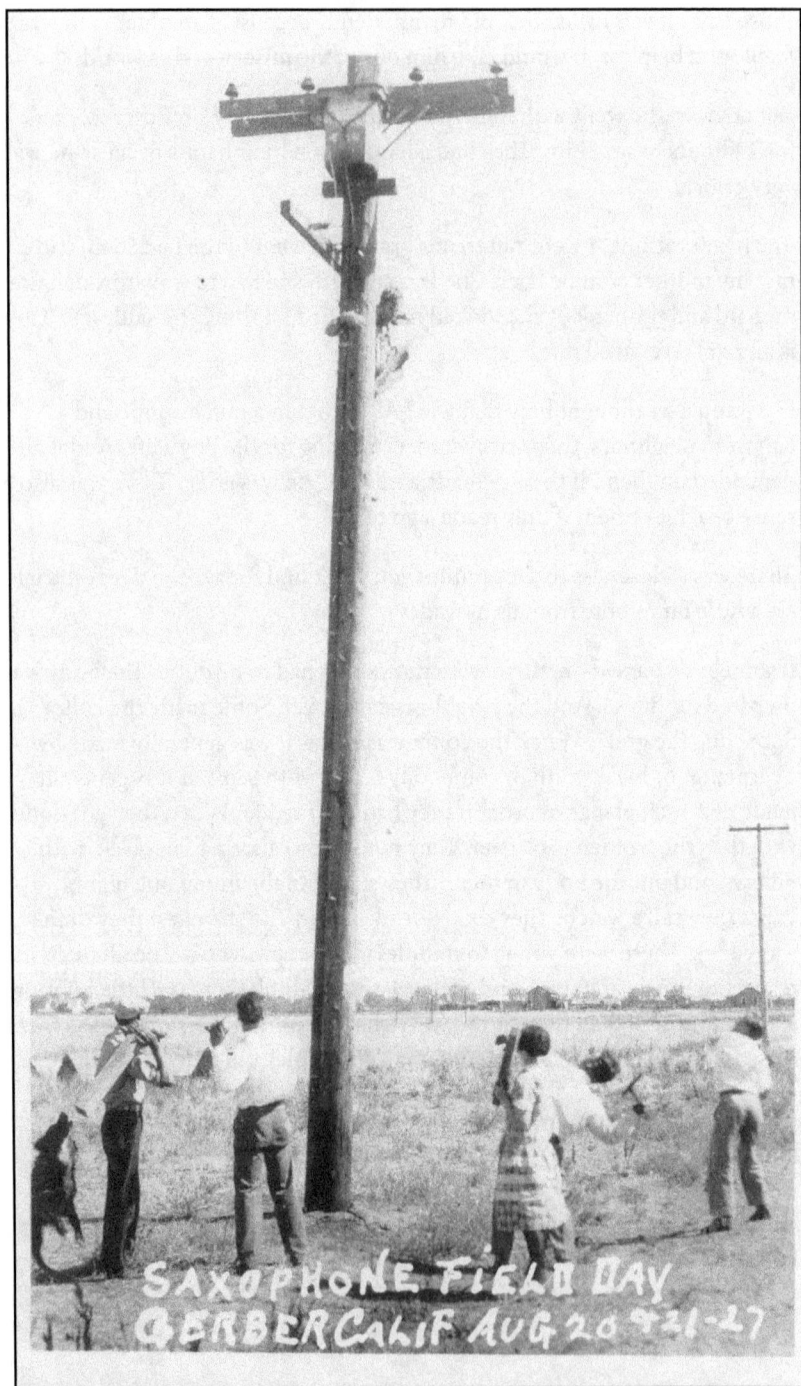

SAXOPHONE FIELD DAY
GERBER CALIF AUG 20 *21-27

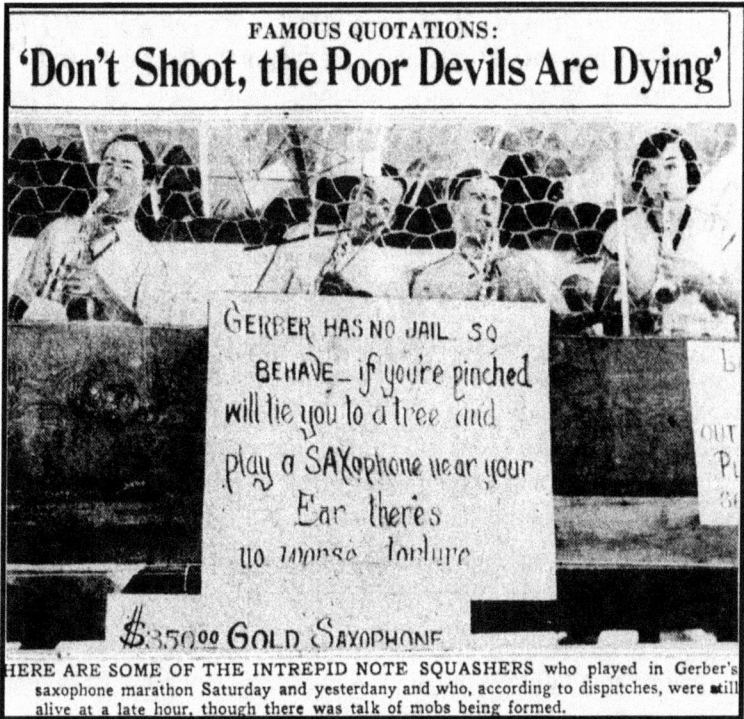

FAMOUS QUOTATIONS:

'Don't Shoot, the Poor Devils Are Dying'

GERBER HAS NO JAIL SO
BEHAVE — if you're pinched
will lie you to a tree and
play a SAXophone near your
Ear there's
no worse torture

$350.00 GOLD SAXOPHONE

HERE ARE SOME OF THE INTREPID NOTE SQUASHERS who played in Gerber's saxophone marathon Saturday and yesterdany and who, according to dispatches, were still alive at a late hour, though there was talk of mobs being formed.

Gerber's 1927 Saxophone Field Day

Josie Reifschneider-Smith

If music is the language of love, a saxophone player hates everybody. (*Red Bluff Daily News* June 3, 1922)

Percival O'Moan, who plans to take part in the saxophone track meet at Gerber, was presented with a coat of mail and a $50,000 accident policy at a farewell party given by friends. Mrs. O'Moan, who has heard Percival practicing, says she hasn't decided yet how she will spend the $50,000. (*San Francisco Examiner* July 31, 1927)

The program will include a barbecue—of cattle, not saxophonists. (*San Francisco Examiner* June 17, 1927)

A Sacramento paper has suggested that the event be held in jail. There is no jail in Gerber, the usual punishment being to tie the offenders to street posts just previous to one of the concerts. Three concerts are figured equal to a life sentence. (*Gerber Star* 1927)

Gerber, Calif., staged a "saxophone field day" without a single murder, which shows the tolerance of folks in the Golden State. (*Henryetta Daily Free-Lance* [Oklahoma] August 25, 1927)

A California town had a saxophone field day with 500 entrants—now how in the world can you blame the climate for that? (*East Hampton Star* [New York] November 11, 1927)

Tooting Its Own Horn

Sometimes history turns up in the unlikeliest of places. Take this photo, for example, that I had seen on eBay. It shows a man with a saxophone up a telephone pole with a barking dog and an unfriendly mob below holding, and about to hurl, bats, rocks, and even a hammer. This postcard languished on eBay for about a year before I finally bought it on a whim. When it came, I put it aside and frankly forgot about it. That was, until I found a brief newspaper clipping and learned that Gerber held a two-day "Saxophone Field Day" (or "Saxophone Rodeo") August 20 and 21, 1927.

Intrigued, I began looking through newspaper archives for more information about this event. I didn't think I'd find much, but I was wrong. This event was publicized throughout the United States and Canada in newspapers large and small, covered by the United Press, and filmed by international newsreel and film companies such as Pathé News, Metro-Goldwyn, Universal, Fox Film, and Paramount Pictures News. It put Gerber on the world's radar for several months. So who was behind this crazy idea?

A MUSICIAN OF NOTE

THE LOWERPHONE

William N. Lower

Music Man William N. Lower

William Lower was born in New York State, 1878, and began the study of music at four years of age, mastering the coronet. At eight, he studied the clarinet; by ten, he entered professional life. He played big time vaudeville all over the United States before coming to California in 1914 to work in the movie industry. He transcribed the music for D. W. Griffith's 1915 movie Birth of a Nation and worked in many other movies.

Lower moved to Gerber in 1926 and started the Gerber Silver Saxophone Band. With 29 members, it was the only exclusive saxophone band in the United States. The band was invited to the 1928 Pasadena Rose Parade and football game (Red Bluff Daily News July 16, 1927). Thanks to his musical enthusiasm, it was estimated that 1 in 20 Gerber area residents played the saxophone. (Lower was also the band leader for the Orland Municipal Band.)

Lester Lafferty of the *Gerber Star*

The idea's "EUREKA!" moment is related in this anecdote published by the *Dayton Daily News* from Ohio:

> Gerber, nestled unromantically in the bosom of Northern California's hop-growing district, always had been considered a peace-loving community, disdainful of things blatant or discordant. The town hankered after nothing and apparently got what it wanted.
>
> That is, until a recent foregathering of a group of boys with warm blood in their veins and a lot of excess wind in their lungs. Gerber, they agreed, must do something—something different— that the world might take cognizance of its existence. But what to do?
>
> Across the night air, vying rather unsatisfactorily with the shunting engines down at the round-house—they change the train engines at Gerber—came the sound of "Fat" Latham's saxophone. This was practice night, quite palpably.
>
> "Gosh!" expostulated one of the disciples of "Do Something," "that guy never runs out of breath, does he?"
>
> That was fate's keynote. Lester Lafferty jumped into the air, clicked his heels, and let out a whoop. "I've got it!" he shouted, and the boys strained to see just what it was he'd "got."
>
> "A saxophone marathon! We'll hold a field day for these daffy tuba blowers. We'll give 'em a chance to blow their heads off. Maybe we'll get rid of some of them that way."
>
> And so the world's first saxophone marathon was brought into being. (September 11, 1927)

Inviting the World

Lower, together with Lafferty (publisher of the *Gerber Star* and *Biggs News* newspapers and Gerber Chamber of Commerce secretary), mailed notices to the "city press" in San Francisco to start the publicity campaign. Newspapers far and wide ran with the story. It succeeded beyond anyone's wildest dreams. From all points in the United States and Canada, entrants came.

Sacramento Bee (July 21, 1927): This city is rapidly winning a reputation of devising ingenious means of self-inflicted punishment. First it organized the saxophone band—the only one in the state. Next it developed the Saxophone Field Day. And now a saxophone marathon with "Yes! We Have No Bananas" the piece de resistance of the endurance event.

The contest starts at noon, August 20th, and the player who survives "No Bananas" and angry citizens will be awarded a gold saxophone.

Riverside Daily News (June 23, 1927 & July 12, 1927): A free barbecue, lunch, and entertainment will be provided, the only admission being a saxophone and the ability to play it. Arrangements have been made with a Pathé film man to take movies of the group.

Gerber bossie giving milk despite saxophone players. (postcard from author's collection)

The baseball diamond will be used to sound off the concert, and a parade of players with their instruments will take place between the town and the ball park.

The "Om-pah-om-om-pah" boys will have the time of their lives with ample police protection from any riots or bloodshed. This little Sacramento valley town, that originated the saxophone band, has a population of but 800, but the saxophone population on that day will probably match the town population.

Bricks, shotguns, shillalahs [clubs], and other implements will be combed from the city prior to the start of the marathon so that the test will be purely physical and spiritual rather than a survival of threatened violence from outsiders. The suggestion has been made that the contestants be placed in some brick-proof structure. Others point out, however, that this little city of 800 people, being a railroad terminal, has acquired hardened eardrums and can withstand the moaning melodies.

Portsmouth [**Ohio**] *Daily Times* (August 19, 1927): Just as dirt is matter out of place, so noise may be music out of place. The sweet notes of the saxophone may be noise to the outer world, but to Gerber, they are heavenly music. How happy Gerber would be if it could have all the saxophone players of this great nation within its gates. And how happy it might make much of the American public outside of Gerber.

Suburban-Magnet [Brookfield, Illinois] (August 19, 1927): Gerber, Calif., is putting itself on the map by holding a Saxophone Field Day. They have invited all the saxophonists in the country and we hope they will all attend—and lose the stub end of their round-trip tickets. The Gerberites say that 500 saxophonists have already promised to be on hand and will put on a program of "music" with "plenty of pep, punch, and percussion," such as "for fulsomeness and energy has never been heard of before." Fulsome is the right word for it.

Both jazz and regular pieces will be played as well as a number of extremely clever novelty pieces, including an "almost perfect imitation of Scotch bagpipes and an amusing German street band." Imagine anyone trying to imitate a Scotch bagpipe—the original is bad enough—but then a man who will travel to California to play a saxophone is liable to do most anything.

They are threatening to make it a national event; isn't there some law that can be invoked to compel them to quarantine it and keep it at home?

San Francisco Examiner (June 17, 1927): Through the medium of radio, Tehama County threatens to inflict upon the world one of its greatest calamities. Five hundred saxophone players are preparing to gather on the baseball diamond and broadcast an imitation of bagpipes playing "The Campbells Are Coming."

Over 500 saxophone players from Canada and all corners of the United States, lugging saxophones great and small, soprano and basso, planned to descend on Gerber to enjoy two days of events.

Gerber Gets Ready

Two blocks, which included the local ball park, were enclosed, and in the center of the field, a platform (the "Cage") screened with brick-proof wire to protect the sax players ("gobblers") was erected for the marathon. The winner of the marathon would receive a gold E flat alto Conn saxophone valued at $350. This and other prizes (totaling $2,000) were displayed in the window of the Cone & Kimball department store in Red Bluff. A Nash sedan was also given away at a drawing held Sunday night. Jim Camp, well-known Gerber train transfer man, was the lucky winner of the car.

Field Day Events and Contests

Befitting such an event, there was a contest for "Queen of the Saxophone Field Day." Mrs. Hattie Walstrom won the title while Miss Evelyn Hoschler was second runner up.

As an added attraction, a baseball game was played between all-star teams from Shasta and Tehama counties. The Shasta team was chosen from Redding and Anderson teams in the Lassen View League; the Tehama team was selected from Gerber, Los Molinos, and Corning teams. The line-up for the Tehama team was Germain (Gerber), c; Joiner (Los Molinos), pitcher; Dent (Los Molinos), 1b; Mundorff (Los Molinos), 2b; Bryan (Los Molinos), 3b; Mellon (Corning), Fifield (Los Molinos), and Hoff (Gerber), outfielders.

Field Day contests included which player came from the longest distance away, best and worst saxophone player (the latter won a leather medal), best quartet, best trio, best duet, oldest and youngest saxophone player,

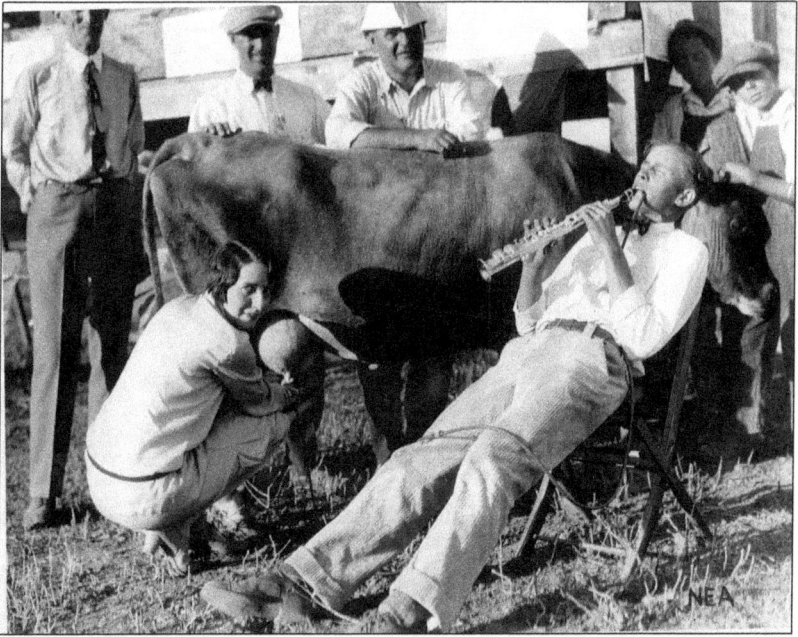

Winning an endurance record in a saxophone marathon at Gerber, Calif., by playing "Yes! We Have No Bananas" for 18 hours and four minutes without stopping, Al Germain of Gerber is shown obtaining sustenance without stopping for it. In order not to miss a bleat of the tune, a rubber tube was connected to a cow on one end and Germain's mouth on the other, and a girl milked the cow. (NEA press photograph, author's collection)

best looking male and female saxophone player, and races in which runners had to play a saxophone the entire distance without missing a note (men's 100-yard dash, women's 50-yard dash, hurdle race, couple race, mile race). There was even a broad jump event, a parade, and, on Sunday, a saxophone throwing contest where:

> grown men will attempt to outdo each other in pitching a saxophone with the bell filled with lead. If the horn hits a 'gobbler' and kills him, the thrower will be given a free ticket to the inquest. As the mouthpiece gobblers start to arrive, their horns [should] be taken in hand, and the bell of each filled with lead. As a token of our sincerity, we offer to close up shop and furnish the committee with our next year's supply of molten linotype metal, which would be ample to plug up a good many horns. (*Red Bluff Daily News* August 18, 1927)

Daily Schedule of Events

Saturday, August 20:

> 10 a.m.—Registration of visiting Saxophonists.
>
> 11:30 a.m.—Instructions to entrants in the marathon contest.
>
> 12 noon—Start of the 24-hour marathon.
>
> 3:15 p.m.—Concert by Gerber Band.
>
> 4 p.m.—Assembling of all saxophonists on grounds.
>
> 4:30 p.m.—Introduction of a new song, "California, the Golden State," sung by Clara Barnett. Words by Miss Laura Mae O'Brien of Vina. Music by W. N. Lower of Gerber.
>
> 5:00 p.m.—Triat heat of Saxophone Throwing Contest.
>
> 6:00 p.m. —Band concert.
>
> 9:00 p.m. —Dance at Rock-A-Bye Pavilion.

Sunday, August 21:

> 11:30 a.m.—Preparing for closing of marathon.
>
> 12 noon—Marathon ends. Barbecue.
>
> 3:00 p.m.—Judging of Best Saxophonist, Worst Saxophonist, Best Looking Male Saxophonist, Best Looking Female Saxophonist.

The celebrated Gerber Silver Saxophone Band. All instruments were from the Conn company and the band gave concerts throughout California. (*Conn Musical Truth* Fall 1927)

4:00 p.m.—Saxophone Throwing Contest.

5:00 p.m.—A rendition of "Yes! We Have No Bananas" by the massed saxophones of 500 addicts.

6:00 p.m.—Closing of race for Queen.

8:00 p.m.—Turkey dinner. Free drawing for a Nash sedan.

Participants

Thirty-nine sax players signed up for the two-day marathon. They included Marcellers Wanee (Richfield), Rudolph Brodnasky (Los Molinos), Albert A. Germain (Gerber), Thaddeus Vinson (Gerber), Frank J. Germain (Gerber), Chas. C. Nickles (Gerber), Freeman Smith (Gerber), Dr. C. C. Bihler (Orland), Alda Bihler (Orland), Erma Bihler (Orland), Spencer

Three Gerber saxophonologists that participated were (top to bottom) Opal Countryman, Pearl Freeman, and Laura Reynolds. (*Sacramento Bee* August 20, 1927)

Bihler (Orland) who played the smallest saxophone made—an E flat soprano sax, Frank Zumwalt (Gerber), Pearl Freeman (Gerber), Clifford Ross (Gerber), C. V. Foss (Gerber), Laura Reynolds (Gerber), Bertha Miller (Red Bluff), Don Honodel (Chico), Don Ashman (Willows), Frank Sawyer (Merced), Frank Kalasek (Denver), Harry Leavitt (Seattle), and representing the San Francisco Conn Company store was L. W. Brewster and Al Hyndman.

Others who helped manage the event were Messrs. Vinson Countryman, Gertsch, Langenwalter, Anderline, Cottar, and the Smith brothers.

From San Francisco and Oakland came Daniel Miller (president, who signed up for the saxophone throwing contest), L. W. Brewster (manager), and Al Hyndman (head salesman) from the San Francisco store of Conn Company (instrument makers), and Mr. and Mrs. Roberts of the Oakland store.

The Marathon

Rules required that each player had to use both hands and their mouth in the contest. A player who took time out to "wet his whistle" was charged double for the time taken.

Judges were on hand to make sure marathoners adhered to the rules. They could play "Yes! We Have No Bananas," "The Prisoner's Song," "Yankee Doodle Dandy," "Here Comes the Bride," and other pieces. They could also run up and down the scale, but all had to stay on a tune or scale and play continuously. If they stopped, they had to signal the timekeeper; if they stopped without signaling, they were disqualified.

Saturday, August 20, 1927

GERBER IS IN THROES OF SAX BAND

Marathon Got Away at 2 p.m. and
Will Wind Up Tomorrow.

Gerber has been without a civic anthem since the town was
established but it is making up for lost time. William Lower's
saxophone marathonists are drilling it into every inhabitant of
the railroad town today and visitors are going away with a vacant
stare in their eyes and mumbling to themselves, "Yes, we have no
bananas." It is a pitiful sight. The saxophonists are grimly battling
fatigue as they continue to toot.

It is reported that the Cascade Limited began to rock and
buckle as it approached the terminal today, throwing a panic into
the tourists. It was later found that vibrations emanating from the
Gerber ball park, which sounding something like the "banana"
song were responsible. If the playing of a violin can rock a bridge,
then a saxophone band can move mountains. (*Red Bluff Daily News*
August 20, 1927)

SAXOPHONES? THROW, BLOW 'EM AT GERBER: LASSEN TREMBLES AMID SCREECHES, YELLS

This village, hitherto known chiefly as the home of the State
Champion lady hog-caller [note: this was Mrs. Andrew Jackson
of Las Flores], startled the countryside today with the first "and
probably the last" saxophone field day with two score unmasked
arpeggio thugs in competition. The first blue notes in the
saxophone playing enduring contest shattered the afternoon heat
waves at 2:30 o'clock.

The first casualty was reported at 2:21 p.m. when Daisy, an
aggressive goat owned by Mrs. Laura Reynolds of the Gerber
Saxophone Band, broke loose from its picket pin and reached the
nearest player.

Residents of Gerber who have endured rehearsals for the
field day cheered today as Daisy picked her man and butted him
squarely in the middle for the gamut. He missed two notes but
went bravely on.

The misery of the marathon continued throughout the afternoon. While other events on the program were being run off, eight men were officially entered in the saxophone throwing contest.

Trial heats for the 100-yard dash for men playing the saxophone and the 50-yard dash for women saxophone players were scheduled for this afternoon but were postponed until tomorrow so that the committee can arrange to hold them in a secluded spot where the entrants will not be forced to run more than the stated distance. It is still uncertain if they would run the gamut or the gauntlet.

Contests to decide on the best saxophone player and the worst saxophone player are set for tomorrow afternoon. The committee went into session tonight to determine on a method of telling the two contests apart.

Reports coming in from the back country indicate the effects of the musical melee are being felt at a wide distance. Mount Lassen, 42 miles away, was reported ready to erupt with rage.

Local interest centers on the three women entrants who will appear on the card tomorrow: Mrs. Robert Stryker (Los Molinos), Miss Alda Bihler (Orland), and Miss Bertha Muller (Redding). They will compete in the 50-yard saxophone-carrying dash for ladies and in the saxophone beauty contest. (*San Francisco Chronicle* August 21, 1927)

Sunday, August 21, 1927

SUFFERIN' CATFISHES!
We Have No Bananas—But We Have Ears!

The Gerber saxophone marathon is on its way. The moaning, squeaking, barking, biting, slippery, peelin'ed tune of "Yes! We Have No Bananas" was the tune allotted to the final contestants by W. M. Lower, head of the Gerber Saxophone Band, for the marathon contest in which the players were to squeal their bananas until they drop, or blow up.

At 10 o'clock last night, after three "heats" of two hours each, the judges called the race off for the night and at 6 o'clock this morning, 10 of the contestants, who finished with their wits still together last night, are to start all over again telling about their bananas until the pavilion on which they have been "caged" falls beneath the vibration or until the lips of the players crystallize. Around the cage were hung a number of placards carrying humorous messages to and about the players—

"Don't tease the saxophone players."

"Don't blow smoke down the saxophone horns. It makes the players sneeze and that only prolongs the agony."

"Please don't throw rocks at the players."

"Don't make faces at the players. They can't laugh and play at the same time."

"Gerber has no jail. If you're pinched, you will be tied to a tree and someone will play a saxophone in your ear. There is no worse torture, so behave." (*The Red Bluff Morning Times*, August 21, 1927)

'Sax' Marvels, Winners on One Count Each

This photograph, taken at Gerber, Calif., shows IDA BIHLER and CORNELIUS HER-MANN, saxophone players par excellence, according to the judges in a recent contest held at that place. They outshone other entrants in a saxophone marathon. Ida was adjudged the prettiest contestant and Cornelius was handed the palm by the judges as being the best player who participated.
(Paramount news photot)

Finally, at 4:04 p.m. Sunday afternoon, the marathon mercifully ended when Al "Biz" Germain outlasted his remaining opponent, Clifford Ross (El Camino), and was declared the winner after playing non-stop for 10 hours that day (8 hours the previous day). The *San Francisco Examiner* and *Sacramento Bee* reported the final moments:

> **San Francisco Examiner** (August 22, 1927): The moaning is over. The Gerber Silver Saxophone Band is out of its misery. Al Germain of Gerber, soprano saxophone soloist, was declared the winner.
>
> At 4:04 p.m., the judge who had been listening intently with bowed head and tears streaming down his cheeks to the notes of Clifford Ross, the sole remaining competitor, lifted his hands and blew a shrill whistle. The sound sent a shiver through taut-nerved Gerber—sleepless and unstrung through the night.
>
> "Mr. Ross has flatted his 'G,'" announced the judge. That was the rule. The first sour note disqualified him and Ross was carried fainting from the fortress in which the saxophonologists had played. Germain was borne away in triumph by the few friends he has left.

> **Sacramento Bee** (August 22, 1927): Silence reigns in this railroad center—a welcome silence after two days made hideous by the concerted efforts of a score of saxophone players trying to outwind each other in the endurance marathon of the Gerber Saxophone Rodeo marathon. Yesterday, Al Germain, sturdy Gerber contractor, was claimed the winner of the contest after 18 hours and 4 minutes of playing out of a possible 24 hours.
>
> Eighteen had entered the contest Saturday noon. By 6 o'clock three had dropped out and at 10 o'clock two more were down for the count. The rest were groggy and the judges at the breaking point. It was decided to take a recess until early morning for the benefit of players, judges, and those who might be trying to sleep in town.
>
> Seven entered yesterday morning of whom Alda Bihler, Clifford Ross, Freeman Smith, Spencer Bihler, and Al Germain stayed until noon. Spencer dropped out from a severe nosebleed.

Miss Bihler took time out three times as her fingers became numb. At noon the contest was scheduled to end but Clifford Ross, Al Germain, and Freeman Smith to this time had no time off and their actual playing time was equal. The judges disqualified all other contestants and allowed these three competitors to continue playing.

They were ordered to play "Yes! We Have No Bananas" in unison, the first player sounding a sour note to be disqualified. At 1:30, Freeman Smith dropped out. Then began a gruelsome battle for endurance between Germain and Ross. For hours they had played the banana ditty without missing a note and without having the mouthpiece of their saxophone from their lips. The crowd pressed against the stand as judges listened.

Three newscameramen took scenes both days of the marathon and as they attempted to take a single of Germain, he refused to pose unless Ross was included in the picture. The winner's prize was a $350 gold saxophone. Second place had no prize.

The *Dayton Daily News* (September 11, 1927) cheekily observed that the "judges died soon" after the marathon ended and that "not since the first Armistice Day has Gerber celebrated as it celebrated the end of that saxophone contest. Even the churches joined in and there were prayers of gratitude offered up."

Other Contest Winners

Cornelius Hermann (Galveston, Texas) won the prize for the best saxophone player. Alda Bihler (Orland) was judged best looking female saxophone player

Charlie Hall got the prize for throwing a saxophone the farthest. "Charlie lives near the ball park, the scene of the fracas. His only regrets were that he couldn't get a chance at every darned sax on the grounds. Probably some of them would have landed in the Sacramento River if Charlie had gotten his clutches on the blamed things" (*Red Bluff Daily News* August 22, 1927). The sax used in the throwing contest was presented to Jim Camp who won the drawing for the Nash sedan.

Afterwards

Despite the optimism of making this an annual event, and to the relief of the nation, it never happened. The following year, William Lower organized a 20-piece saxophone band in Cottonwood—the Cottonwood Band of Shasta County. They held a one-day "second" Saxophone Field Day in Cottonwood on Labor Day Monday in 1928. "In the saxophone marathon contest, Melvin Heer won the first prize ($75) and Miss Bacon of Jellys Ferry won the second prize ($25)" (*Red Bluff Morning Times* September 6, 1928).

The Gerber Silver Saxophone Band fades away in the newspapers. However, the "William N. Lower Band" did play for the 1928 Red Bluff Round-Up, which is celebrating it's Centenary this year. ◎

SUNSET HOMESEEKERS' BUREAU OF INFORMATION

TEHAMA COUNTY
CALIFORNIA

COUNTY BRIDGE ACROSS SACRAMENTO RIVER

Mild Climate, Good Soil, Ample Rainfall, Unsurpassed Scenery, Varied Industries

Deciduous and Citrus Fruits, Alfalfa, Wool, Lumber, Grain

A Great Irrigation Project now contemplated

Write to the Secretary Chamber of Commerce, Red Bluff, California

Newspaper boys ("newsies") in St. Louis, Missouri, 11 a.m. Monday morning, May 9, 1910. Lewis Wickes Hine photographer; Library of Congress.

The Deadly Cigarette: Greatest Evil of Modern High School

"Men frequently injured by smoking and boys always. Exposed to the cold and wet, they find that it warms them up."
(Horaltio Alger, *Ragged Dick*, 1868)

☙

Modern-day e-cigarettes are hand-held battery-powered devices that heat a liquid containing nicotine and flavorings to create a vapor that a user inhales (or "vapes") instead of smokes. First patented in 1963 (but not a commercial success), they became successful in 2004 when the first modern e-cigarette was patented. By 2014, *Oxford Dictionary's* word-of-the-year was "vape."

Concerns for health risks, manufacture of devices, electronic waste, and, in particularly, questionable marketing practices geared toward young adults and teens has led to increased government regulation. However, the old adage "everything old is new again" is certainly true in this case when you look back to the turn of the 20th century and the war on childhood smoking.

In an urban or inner city environment during the later 1800s, many children who were unsupervised, worked long hours to help support their families, or lived and hustled on the streets to survive smoked. Mass-production of cigarettes in the 1800s made them readily available.

In the early 1900s, there was a nationwide effort to pass legislation to make smoking cigarettes by minors illegal. Cigarettes were considered more dangerous than cigars or pipes: they were considered milder, which would make inhaling the smoke easier to do. Some people felt the papers used for cigarette manufacture were unhealthy or that cigarettes could be used as a gateway to illicit drug abuse.

While the national effort failed, several states developed legislation to combat underage smoking. California Governor Gillett signed legislation in 1909 that made it possible for boys under 18 to be arrested for cigarette smoking. Juvenile violators wouldn't be put in jail but placed under the control of probation officers and, "when necessary, confined in reform schools" (current law forbids tobacco sales to anyone under 21 years of age).

The dangers of cigarette smoking were published in newspapers far and wide. Parents and school authorities were encouraged to get involved and push for more legislation to stop underage smoking. In Tehama County, a very vocal proponent was Red Bluff High School principal Paul Ward, who warned of the dangers of cigarette smoking during school assemblies and interviews with local newspapers. His statistics were quoted by many as proof that cigarette smoking needed to be regulated. As he was quoted:

> *Loafing around pool rooms is not the only evil or perhaps the worst that the High School boys indulge in. I believe the cigarette habit is the greatest handicap in existence against the high school boy. High school is failing in its work with the boys largely because of the use of tobacco.*

> *High School is the most critical period of the boy's life: the adolescent period when he is changing from a boy to a man, and that to take up the tobacco habit at this period would almost certainly nullify any effort made with his studies. He urged that if they wished to use tobacco, they should wait until this critical period was passed. He made no claims that the use of tobacco was particularly harmful to the ordinary man nor did he criticize him for using it, but he accused the teaching profession of Northern California of a*

low standard of ethics. A teacher should be a model example to the boys along the tobacco and liquor lines and no man addicted to the use of tobacco or alcoholic drinks would be added to the faculty of the Red Bluff High School.

There have been volumes of stuff printed to show why the boy quits school. Every such volume should have the picture of a cigarette as its frontispiece. Tobacco, worse than any other factor, is responsible for those boys who fall by the wayside.

The High School Record Book containing records of every boy who has been enrolled in the school during the past eight years was brought before the school and the records of tobacco users laid bare to the public gaze. These records contained some startling information: Not a single high school boy in the last eight years and probably in the history of the school who has been addicted to the use of tobacco has graduated from Red Bluff High School with sufficient credit to give him entrance to the university.

Records of 69 boys enrolled between the years of 1902 and 1908 showed that 32 used tobacco, which meant about half the boys in high school use tobacco. During this time, our school has graduated from its four-year course 15 non-tobacco users (12 recommended for scholarship and 11 going to higher institutions of learning) and only six tobacco users. Of these six, three took five years to finish and then finish badly.

I have been in charge of various California schools for the past eighteen years, most of the time being supervising principal of both grammar school and high school, and invariably in my experience the tobacco boy, if he ever reached the high school, did so in a weakened condition. Never, in those eighteen years, have I graduated a tobacco boy from the high school with sufficient credit to gain entrance to the state university. Not one of them has ever made any serious effort towards a higher education. Such boys are like wormy apples. They drop long before the harvest time. Very few of them ever advance far enough to enter college. Very few of those who enter last beyond the first year. They rarely make failures in after life because they do not have any after life. The boy who begins cigarette smoking before he is 15, never enters the life of the world. When other boys are taking hold of the world's work, he is concerned with the sexton and undertaker. There is one grim argument to be made for the use of cigarettes by boys—it helps on the survival of the fittest. The manly boy does not take to such things.

The whole school course is strewn with tobacco wrecks.

But if every school man would dig up the local records that lie right before him and publish them to his school and to his town he cannot fail. The three Red Bluff dailies were eager for the data we offered. Many papers throughout the state copied it. The boys were impressed. The percentage of tobacco boys in the Red Bluff high school fell, in one year, from forty-six per cent to less than ten per cent.

Out of the 42 boys enrolled in the Red Bluff school during the year just closed, only four are using tobacco habitually. Two of these, although they have been with us for three years, have done less than two years of work, and have done that badly. As far as getting an education is concerned, they are hopelessly lost. The other two are deficient in their work and will only help to swell the records against tobacco.

The Red Bluff records can in all probability be duplicated in any high school in California.

The people stand behind any movement against the tobacco evil. So do the newspapers. The legislature has done what it could. It is your time at the bat, Mr. Schoolman, and here's to you for a "good eye" and a "safe hit." ◉

(Compiled from several local Red Bluff newspapers columns/editorials from 1910.)

Breeching: Coming of Age

Unbreeching, the custom of dressing small boys in frocks (e.g., dresses, gowns), started in the mid-16th century and continued until the very early 20th century. The reasons were 1) economics (clothes were expensive so it made sense to dress very young children in outfits that allowed for their growth or in hand-me-downs of both sexes), and 2) practicality (changing diapers and toilet training was much faster and easier without having to deal with the complicated buttons and fastening of regular boys' clothes).

Leslie Freeman, age 4, c. 1895
(unbreeched)

Jesse E. Campbell, age 7, c. 1893
(breeched)

Breeching was the first time a little boy began wearing short trousers (or breeches), which still allowed for growth and were cheaper than long trousers. In the 19th century, this usually occurred between the ages of four and seven. It was a special occasion celebrated by friends and family because the change in dress signified that the little boy was now a young man.

- Ashelford, Jane. 1996 *The Art of Dress: Clothing and Society, 1500-1914*. Abrams.
- Baumgarten, Linda. 2002. *What Clothes Reveal: The Language of Clothing in Colonial and Federal America*. Yale University Press.
- Frost, Natasha. 2017. "For Centuries, People Celebrated a Little Boy's First Pair of Trousers." https://www.atlasobscura.com/articles/breeching-party-first-pants-regency-trousers-boys.
- Photos from the Tehama County Library archives.